Revised and Updated Second Edition!

Business Model YOU

The One-Page Way to Reinvent Your Work at Any Life Stage

Published by John Wiley & Sons, Inc., Hoboken, New Jersey. Published simultaneously in Canada.

All cases in this book involve actual clients of the authors or Business Model You® Certified Practitioners personally trained by the authors. For privacy reasons, in some instances names, photographs, or case details have been changed. For educational purposes, in some instances dialogue or circumstances have been reimagined.

For general information on our other products and services or for technical support, please contact our Customer Care Department within the United States at (800) 762-2974, outside the United States at (317) 572-3993 or fax (317) 572-4002.

Wiley also publishes its books in a variety of electronic formats. Some content that appears in print may not be available in electronic formats. For more information about Wiley products, visit our website at www.wiley.com.

Library of Congress Cataloging-in-Publication Data

Names: Clark, Tim, 1956- author. | Hazen, Bruce, author. | Osterwalder, Alexander, author. | Pigneur, Yves, author. | Smith, Alan, 1982- author. | John Wiley & Sons, publisher.

Title: Business model you : the one-page way to reinvent your work at any life stage / written by Tim Clark and Bruce Hazen, in collaboration with Alexander Osterwalder, Yves Pigneur, and Alan Smith.

Description: Revised and updated second edition. | Hoboken, New Jersey : Wiley, [2023] | Includes index.

Identifiers: LCCN 2022036503 (print) | LCCN 2022036504 (ebook) | ISBN 9781119879640 (paperback) | ISBN 9781119879664 (adobe pdf) | ISBN 9781394152278

Subjects: LCSH: Career development. | Success in business.

Classification: LCC HF5381 .C6597 2023 (print) | LCC HF5381 (ebook) | DDC 650.1--dc23/eng/20220906

LC record available at https://lccn.loc.gov/2022036503

LC ebook record available at https://lccn.loc.gov/2022036504

Cover Illustration: Matt Hammill, modified by Keiko Onodera with permission

Designed by Keiko Onodera and Alan Smith with additional illustrations and photographs by Keiko Onodera

SKY10035753_091622

Revised and Updated Second Edition!

Business Model YOU

The One-Page
Way to Reinvent
Your Work at
Any Life Stage

Written by
Tim Clark and Bruce Hazen
in collaboration with
Alexander Osterwalder,
Yves Pigneur, and Alan Smith

WILEY

How Business Model You® Started

Tim

In 2009 author Tim Clark began applying entrepreneurship and design thinking principles to career development using the groundbreaking Business Model Canvas developed by Alexander Osterwalder and Yves Pigneur.

Alex

Yves

Adie Shariff
Afroz Ali
AJ Shah
Alan Scott
Alan Smith
Alejandro Lembo
Alessandro De Sanctis
Alexander Osterwalder
Alfredo Osorio Asenjo
Ali Heathfield
Allan Moura Lima
Allen Miner
Amber Lewis
Andi Roberts
Andre Malzoni dos Santos Dias
Andrew E. Nixon
Andrew Warner
Anne McCrossan
Annemarie Ehren
Annette Mason
Ant Clay

Anthony Caldwell
Anthony Moore
Anton de Gier
Anton de Wet
Antonio Lucena de Faria
Beau Braund
Ben Carey
Ben White
Bernd Nurnberger
Bernie Maloney
Bertil Schaart
Björn Kijl
Blanca Vergara
Bob Fariss
Brenda Eichelberger
Brian Ruder
Brigitte Roujol
Bruce Hazen
Bruce MacVarish
Brunno Pinto Guedes Cruz
Bryan Aulick

Bryan Lubic
Camilla van den Boom
Carl B. Skompinski
Carl D'Agostino
Carles Esquerre Victori
Carlos Jose Perez Ferrer
Caroline Cleland
Cassiano Farani
Catharine MacIntosh
Cesar Picos
Charles W. Clark
Cheenu Srinivasan
Cheryl Rochford
Christian Labezin
Christian Schneider
Christine Thompson
Cindy Cooper
Claas Peter Fischer
Claire Fallon
Claudio D'Ipolitto
Császár Csaba

Daniel E. Huber
Daniel Pandza
Daniel Sonderegger
Danijel Brener
Danilo Tic
Darcy Walters-Robles
Dave Crowther
Dave Wille
David Devasahayam
Edwin
David Hubbard
David Sluis
Deborah Burkholder
Deborah Mills-Scofield
Denise Taylor
Diane Mermigas
Dinesh Neelay
Diogo Carmo
Donald McMichael
Dora Luz González
Bañales

Doug Gilbert
Doug Morwood
Doug Newdick
Dr. Jerry A. Smith
Dustin Lee Watson
Ed Voorhaar
Edgardo Vazquez
Eduardo Pedreño
Edwin Kruis
Eileen Bonner
Elie Besso
Elizabeth Topp
Eltje Huisman
Emmanuel A. Simon
Eric Anthony Spieth
Eric Theunis
Erik A. Leonavicius
Erik Kiaer
Erik Silden
Ernest Buise
Ernst Houdkamp

Eugen Rodel
Evert Jan van Hasselt
Fernando Saenz-Marrero
Filipe Schuur
Floris Kimman
Floris Venneman
Fran Moga
Francisco Barragan
Frank Penkala
Fred Coon
Fred Jautzus
Freek Talsma
Frenetta A. Tate
Frits Oukes
Gabriel Shalom
Gary Percy
Geert van Vlijmen
Gene Browne
Ginger Grant, PhD
Giorgio Casoni
Giorgio Pauletto

Giselle Della Mea
Greg Krauska
Greg Loudoun
Hank Byington
Hans Schriever
Hansrudolf Suter
Heiner Kaufmann
Hind
IJsbrand Kaper
Iñigo Irizar
Ioanna Matsouli
Ivo Frielink
Iwan Müller
Jacco Hiemstra
James C. Wylie
James Fyles
Jan Schmiedgen
Jason Mahoney
Javier Guevara
Jean Gasen
Jeffrey Krames

Jelle Bartels
Jenny L. Berger
Jeroen Bosman
Joeri de Vos
Joeri Lefévre
Johan Ploeg
Johann Gevers
Johannes Frühmann
John Bardos
John van Beek
John Wark
John L. Warren
John Ziniades
Jonas Ørts Holm
Jonathan L. York
Joost de Wit
Joost Fluitsma
Jordi Collell
Juerg H. Hilgarth-Weber
Justin Coetsee
Justin Junier

The result was a pioneering book on "career modeling" called *Business Model You*, created in collaboration with Alexander Osterwalder, Yves Pigneur, Alan Smith, Patrick van der Pijl, Trish Papadakos, and Megan Lacey, with contributions from more than 300 career coaches, human resource professionals, and work wizards from 43 countries, whose names appear here (see their photos on the previous page).

Alan

Trish

Patrick

Megan

Kadena Tate
Kai Kollen
Kamal Hassan
Karin van Geelen
Karl Burrow
Katarzyna Krolak-Wyszynska
Katherine Smith
Keiko Onodera
Keith Hampson
Kevin Fallon
Khushboo Chabria
Klaes Rohde Ladeby
Kuntal Trivedi
Lacides R. Castillo
Lambert Becks
Laura Stepp
Laurence Kuek Swee Seng
Lauri Kutinlahti
Lawrence Traa
Lee Heathfield
Lenny van Onselen

Linda Bryant
Liviu Ionescu
Lukas Feuerstein
Luzi von Salis
Maaike Doyer
Maarten Bouwhuis
Maarten Koomans
Manuel Grassler
Marc McLaughlin
Marcelo Salim
Marcia Kapustin
Marco van Gelder
Margaritis Malioris
Maria Augusta Orofino
Marieke Post
Marieke Versteeg
Marijn Mulders
Marjo Nieuwenhuijse
Mark Attaway
Mark Eckhardt
Mark Fritz

Mark Lundy
Mark Nieuwenhuizen
Markus Heinen
Martin Howitt
Martin Kaczynski
Marvin Sutherland
Mats Pettersson
Matt Morscheck
Matt Stormont
Matthijs Bobeldijk
Megan Lacey
Melissa Cooley
Michael Dila
Michael Eales
Michael Estabrook
Michael Korver
Michael N. Wilkens
Michael S. Ruzzi
Michael Weiss
Mikael Fuhr
Mike Lachapelle

Miki Imazu
Mikko Mannila
Mohamad Khawaja
Natasja la Lau
Nathalie Ménard
Nathan Robert Mol
Nathaniel Spohn
Nei Grando
Niall Daly
Nick Niemann
Nicolas De Santis
Oliver Buecken
Olivier J. Vavasseur
Orhan Gazi Kandemir
Paola Valeri
Patrick Betz
Patrick Keenan
Patrick Quinn
Patrick Robinson
Patrick van der Pijl
Paul Hobcraft

Paul Merino
Paula Asinof
Pere Losantos
Peter Gaunt
Peter Quinlan
Peter Schreck
Peter Sims
Peter Squires
Petrick de Koning
Philip Galligan
Philippe De Smit
Philippe Rousselot
Pieter van den Berg
PK Rasam
Rahaf Harfoush
Rainer Bareiß
Ralf de Graaf
Ralf Meyer
Ravinder S. Sethi
Raymond Guyot
Rebecca Cristina C Bulhoes

Silva
Reiner Walter
Renato Nobre
Riaz Peter
Richard Bell
Richard Gadberry
Richard Narramore
Richard Schieferdecker
Rien Dijkstra
Robert van Kooten
Rocky Romero
Roland Wijnen
Rory O'Connor
Rudolf Greger
Sang-Yong Chung (Jay)
Sara Coene
Scott Doniger
Scott Gillespie
Scott J. Propp
Sean Harry
Sean S. Kohles, PhD

Sebastiaan Terlouw
Shaojian Cao
Simon Kavanagh
Simone Veldema
Sophie Brown
Steve Brooks
Steven Forth
Steven Moody
Stewart Marshall
Stuart Woodward
Sune Klok Gudiksen
Sylvain Montreuil
Symon Jagersma
Tania Hess
Tatiana Maya Valois
Tom Yardley
Thomas Drake
Thomas Klimek
Thomas Røhr Kristiansen
Thorsten Faltings
Tiffany Rashel

Till Kraemer
Tim Clark
Tim Kastelle
Toni Borsattino
Tony Fischer
Travis Cannon
Trish Papadakos
Tufan Karaca
Ugo Merkli
Uta Boesch
Veronica Torras
Vicki Lind
Vincent de Jong
Ying Zhao-Chau
Yves Claude Aubert
Yves Pigneur

Since Business Model You *was released, career modeling has gone global, with the book published in 20 languages. This all-new edition celebrates work re-inventors around the world—including you!*

Bruce

Expert career consultant Bruce Hazen and trainer/coach extraordinaire Mercedes Hoss quickly joined as methodology co-developers as Business Model You® evolved and was adopted by individual professionals and organizations around the world.

Mercedes

"Years after we introduced the Service Model concept from Business Model You®, our nursing leaders continue to use it to reduce organizational ambiguity and create high-functioning teams," says Dana Bjarnason, Vice President and Chief Nursing Executive of Oregon Health Sciences University.

Personal branding guru and long-time collaborator Luigi Centenaro joined us for this all-new edition to teach you how to craft a powerful personal brand.

Luigi

"We find Business Model You® highly useful for training early-career employees how to work effectively within organizations," says Amsterdam-based Marcel Leijen, Director of the ManpowerGroup's Experis Academy.

German

Italian

Portuguese

Czech

Arabic

Farsi

Business Model You® Partners and Certified Practitioners

Sophie

In China, Business Model You® methodology licensee BCC Group, led by founder Sophie He (贺芳芳) and Senior Consultant Jason Du (杜军), trains enterprises and individuals.

Jason

Today more than 600 Business Model You® Certified Practitioners are active worldwide. Find one at BMYDirectory.com—or learn how to become certified at PractitionerTraining.org.

Organizations Using Business Model You®

BASF	EncoreNEO	Hitachi	Owens Corning	Siili
Bayer	Enel	HP	Ping An	Tencent
BCC Group	Experis Academy	Learn2Earner	PWC	
Cattolica	EY	ManpowerGroup	Rabobank	...plus more than 50
China Merchants Bank	Google	OHSU	SAP	universities and colleges
Daiichi Sankyo	Grunenthal	Orange	ServiceMaster	

Russian

Chinese (simplified)

Chinese (traditional)

Korean

Japanese

Mongolian

People Like You

Featured in This Book

Contents

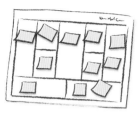

1 Diagram

*Learn to understand and describe workplaces
—and your own work*

2 Reflect

*Revisit your work model
and consider parts that need to change*

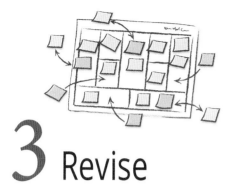

3 Revise

Re-diagram your work model

4 Test

Test your work model

5 Next Steps

Learn how to keep going—and meet the community and resources behind Business Model You®

Diagram

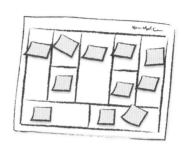

CHAPTER 1

The Key to Workplace Satisfaction and the Cure for Workplace Suffering

A Bigger View of Work

Do you dream about a different way of working? Even a new career?
We all do. But most of us lack a proven, structured way to make fundamental changes in how we work.

Instead, we remain unsatisfied, unfulfilled—maybe even suffering at work—until the pain of staying in place grows stronger than the fear of changing our situation.

This illustrates an uncomfortable truth: most of us take on a more-or-less haphazard series of jobs that, over time and with luck, converge around a general theme. Our careers develop by default rather than by design.

We call this hands-off approach to professional progress "spending your career getting one-job-in-a-row." But rather than getting one-job-in-a-row, most of us would prefer to progress intentionally toward more satisfying work in line with our interests and strengths.

This book shows you exactly how to do that.

You will start by gaining a bigger view of work, using simple, one-page diagrams that visually depict 1) your workplace or customers, and 2) how your personal work benefits them. Seeing diagrams that depict the critical interrelationships between your work and the environment in which you perform it—rather than merely using words to describe work as a collection of tasks—is the heart of our method. This bigger view will widen your influence, wherever or however you work.

Be confident that mastering our method will serve you for a lifetime, because it is based on timeless human principles that remain unchanged regardless of the latest economic ups and downs, technology crazes, socio-political upheavals, or labor market shifts. It will give you a lasting key to workplace satisfaction—and a lifelong cure for workplace suffering.

The following chapters explain everything step-by-step using examples and cases. The book concludes with clear three-step instructions that provide a lifelong navigation tool for negotiating the twists and turns of your professional life. Work through it and you—like hundreds of thousands of worldwide readers of the first edition of *Business Model You*—will discover the tremendous power of modeling. You are now part of a global phenomenon: *Business Model You* has been published in 20 different languages!

Why Business Models?

No doubt you've heard the term "business model" before. What is it, exactly?

At the most basic level, a business model is **the logic by which an organization sustains itself financially**.

As the term suggests, it ordinarily describes businesses. Our approach, though, asks you to consider yourself a one-person enterprise, whether you work in business or a non-commercial field such as government, healthcare, or education. Then, it helps you define and modify your "work model"—including the logic by which you earn your living and how you engage your interests and strengths to grow personally and professionally while delivering benefits to colleagues or clients.

As it turns out, a business model is a potent framework by which to regularly describe, analyze, and change how you work. Think of our method as a perpetually renewable resource for astutely positioning yourself in the world of work throughout your life.

Changing Times, Changing Models

Most of us work by taking jobs with organizations. And the market for those jobs is affected by factors beyond our personal control: new technology, economic booms and busts, sweeping social or demographic trends, intensifying global competition, environmental issues, and so forth.

You saw how the climate change crisis, combined with dramatic improvements in battery and other technologies, accelerated the shift to electric vehicles and power sources, creating entirely new industry sectors and jobs while disrupting corporations and careers too tightly tied to traditional gasoline engines or fossil fuel production.

You witnessed how war and the global COVID pandemic disrupted social and civic life and upended industries, workplaces, and careers. And you've seen for yourself how the highly visible murders of Black Americans forced a social awakening and compelled organizations to take diversity, equity, and inclusion (DEI) seriously in their hiring and promotion practices.

These external factors are beyond the control of both individuals and enterprises—and they profoundly affect how enterprises operate.

Because they can't change the environments in which they operate, enterprises must change their *business models* (and sometimes create new ones) to remain competitive—or even to survive.

As it turns out, these new models themselves disrupt and cause change. In turn, that creates new opportunities for some workers and unemployment for others. New business models continue to alter workplaces and workstyles everywhere, in commercial and non-profit sectors alike.

People Must Change, Too

We're hardly claiming that people are the same as organizations. But here's an important parallel: You, like organizations, are affected by environmental and economic factors beyond your control.

Since you can't control these factors, how can you maintain success and satisfaction? You must identify how you operate, then adapt your approach to fit changing environments.

Just as important as environmental changes are the lifestage changes we all experience as we grow older. People in their early 20s just starting their careers usually have very different life concerns compared to people in their 30s who may be getting married and having children. Similarly, those in their 30s differ from older people who are babysitting grandchildren, getting ready to retire, dealing with death or illness, or embarking on so-called "encore" careers.

Rest assured that the skills you'll learn from *Business Model You* will give you the power to deal artfully with both environmental and lifestage changes.

Personal Work Models for Everyone, Including Healthcare, Education, and Government Workers

One thing we've learned since the first edition of *Business Model You* was released is that the method has proven exactly as useful to non-businesspeople as to businesspeople. That's why we developed service models for use by professionals working in largely non-commercial fields such as government, healthcare, education, and nonprofit or social ventures. While many business and self-help books over-focus on employees of earnings-driven enterprises, our intention is to serve all professionals, whether they are striving for social impact, personal expression, or earnings.

An Ecology of Work

As you get ready to make changes in where, how, or why you work, it can be helpful to step back and take a "macro" view to see work as an ecosystem.

Think of work as a tree: a tree that grows in the rich soil of unchanging human needs such as food, clothing, shelter, health, community, and security. Work, like a tree, has roots, trunk, branches, and leaves.[1]

Leaves are the least durable elements of the tree. When wind blows, leaves scatter and fall. When seasons change, leaves shrivel and die.

Leaves are like **jobs**: the least durable form of work. Each day thousands of old jobs disappear, and thousands of new ones appear.

Branches are more durable than leaves. They bend in the wind and endure changing seasons. But when storms hit, they often break or fall.

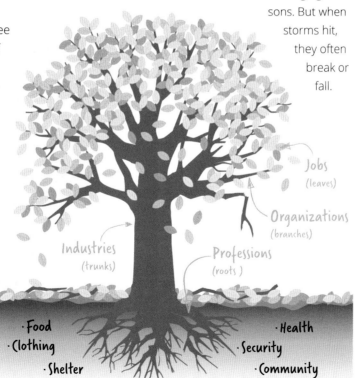

Industries
(trunks)

Jobs
(leaves)

Organizations
(branches)

Professions
(roots)

· Food
· Clothing
· Shelter

· Health
· Security
· Community

Branches are like **organizations**: more durable than leaves, yet only a tiny fraction live longer than a person (statistics show the average lifespan of a company on Standard & Poor's 500 index is just over 21 years).

Trunks are more durable than branches. They defy winds and seasons—even storms. But when fire rages or lightning strikes, they can die.

Tree trunks are like **industries**: far more durable than branches yet given enough time they too may perish. Look what's happened to travel agencies, taxicabs, department stores, and newspapers.

Roots are the most enduring element of a tree. When leaves, branches, and trunks die, roots hold the promise of new life.

Roots are like **professions**: they are the most enduring form of work. Capable people can find other industries in which to practice their professions.

But what exactly does **profession** mean?

In twelfth-century French, the word meant "vows taken upon entering a religious order," and in medieval Latin, "public declaration." Later it came to mean "any solemn declaration" and "occupation one professes to be skilled in."

Today, a profession means a specialized occupation 1) requiring a high level of skill, knowledge, and/or training, and 2) for which there are established paths along which practitioners can progress toward ever greater competency or complexity.

For example, forklift driving is not a profession because there is no path for progressing beyond competently operating a forklift. But welding is a profession because there are multiple paths for progressing to complex materials, applications, and construction environments.

Many people, of course, work outside of professions. They may derive more meaning and satisfaction from family, hobbies, religion, or other nonwork activities than they do from their jobs.[2] But whether people work within a profession or not, the ultimate source of work—the work ecosystem—is the same.

All work grows in the rich soil of unchanging human needs such as food, clothing, shelter, health, community, and security. Work exists and evolves to satisfy one or more of these core needs.

Therefore, the more directly your work involves providing food, shelter, healthcare, or other core needs, the more stable it will be.

The farther removed your work is from addressing basic needs—such as making T-shirts for people who already have everything, or processing documents three tiers removed from finance customers—the less

stable your work will be. Here's a good question to ask ourselves: How directly does our work serve core human needs?

People who focus on getting one **job** after another pursue the least stable form of work. People who stay in one **organization** enjoy greater stability, and those who specialize in an industry enjoy even more. But **professions**, especially those that focus on core human needs, provide the most enduring, stable form of work.

Focus on a profession if you can.

Career Planning Is Dead: Long Live Personal Work Modeling

Traditional career planning emphasized a linear "plan and execute" process starting with a personality and/or vocational assessment and proceeding smoothly to vocation selection, education, long-term employment, then retirement. But this approach has been outmoded for decades—and it is unclear whether it ever worked well for most people.

We prefer a design thinking approach to work, which emphasizes **test and pivot** over **plan and execute**. The traditional plan and execute approach to problem solving looks something like this:

1. Define the problem as quickly as you can
2. Spend lots of time developing a plan for solving the problem
3. Execute the plan
4. Clean up the mess when the plan collides with reality

In contrast, **test and pivot** looks something like this:

1. Spend lots of time defining the problem
2. Imagine many possible solutions, then select the one that arises most naturally
3. Prototype and test that solution
4. Learn from what happens when the prototype collides with reality, then either move forward or pivot (go back to Step 1, 2, or 3)

The key elements of design thinking are defining, ideating, prototyping, and testing. This sequence parallels our four-phase **DIAGRAM > REFLECT > REVISE > TEST** work reinvention process.

Work reinvention, like design thinking, is iterative, meaning you must often repeat one step in the process several times, as when you DIAGRAM a workplace several times until it makes complete sense.

Work reinvention also resembles design thinking in that it is recursive, meaning you may have to return to an earlier phase in the sequence. For example, when **TEST** shows that a new work model clashes with market reality, you must return to the REVISE phase (or even the **REFLECT** phase).

Whew, that is a lot to remember! That's why **DIAGRAMS** are so useful: they show us information and relationships as pictures so we can avoid having to keep too many words in mind.

Now it's time to get started diagramming your work. Use the following pages like a sketchbook: jot down notes, underline key phrases, or doodle in the margins (we pre-spilled coffee here so you won't hesitate to scribble).

Let's go!

CHAPTER 2

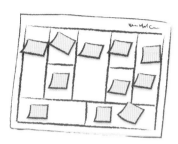

To Understand Your Work, Understand Your Workplace

The Business Model Canvas

We defined *"business model"* as the logic by which an enterprise sustains itself financially. Put simply, *it's the logic by which an enterprise earns its livelihood.*

You might think of a business model as a "blueprint" describing how an organization or team operates.

Just as an architect prepares blueprints to guide construction of a building, an entrepreneur designs a business model to guide the creation of an enterprise. Similarly, a manager might sketch a business model to better understand how an existing organization operates.

To start understanding an existing business model, ask two questions:

1. **Who is the Customer?**
2. **What job does the Customer need to have done?**

To illuminate this idea, let's look at three enterprises.

First: Think about Lyft, the ride-hailing service that lets consumers order and pay for taxicab-like service using their smartphones.

Users of traditional taxicab services and people without cars often find Lyft faster, easier, and less expensive than traditional taxicab services. And because they pay using Lyft's smartphone application, they don't directly pay or tip the driver. That saves time and encourages pleasant interactions between passengers and drivers.

Next, consider Kumon.

Kumon provides after-school mathematics and reading enrichment programs for preschool through high school students. But unlike expensive enrichment programs based on one-to-one tutoring charged by the hour, Kumon supervises students as they work independently on progressive series of worksheets, while their parents pay a modest, fixed monthly charge per subject.

Finally, there's Vesta, a firm that completes electronic purchases on behalf of companies that execute hundreds of thousands of transactions daily. Handling such transactions is complex and demands robust, leading-edge security and anti-fraud measures—two things that few companies can afford to develop and maintain in-house.

So, what do these three businesses have in common?

All receive payment for helping Customers get jobs done.

- Lyft helps passengers arrive more quickly and with greater psychological comfort compared to traditional taxicabs.

- Kumon helps parents who want their children to develop self-discipline and succeed in school.

- Vesta helps businesses eliminate fraud and keep their focus on specialties unrelated to payment collection.

Sounds simple, right?

Well, unlike these examples, defining "**Customers**" and "jobs" in sectors such as government, healthcare, education, and non-profit or social enterprises can be challenging.

A big part of business model thinking is helping you identify and describe both Customers and jobs. Specifically, you'll learn how you can help Customers accomplish the jobs they need to do. And in doing so, you'll discover how to earn more money and gain more satisfaction from your work.

Every Organization Has a Business Model

Since a "business model" is the logic by which an enterprise sustains itself financially, does this mean that only for-profit corporations have business models?

No.

Every enterprise has a business model.[3]

This is true because nearly every modern enterprise, whether for-profit, nonprofit, government, or otherwise, needs money to carry out its work.

For example, imagine you work for Mercy Corps, a nonprofit organization that helps people suffering from poverty or disaster, primarily in emerging nations. Though Mercy Corps is a nonprofit group, it must still:

- Pay staff salaries, facility rent, travel expenses, and utilities

- Purchase equipment and supplies to support its agriculture, emergency response, and other programs

- Provide vouchers or lend money to microbusinesses and aspiring entrepreneurs

- Build a reserve fund for expanding services in the future

Mercy Corps' main motivation is not financial gain; instead, its goal is to serve communities in need. Still, even a nonprofit organization needs cash to carry out its work.

Therefore, like any other enterprise, Mercy Corps **must be paid for helping Customers get jobs done**.

Let's ask our two business model questions about Mercy Corps:

Who Is the Customer?

Mercy Corps actually has two sets of **Customers**. The first set of **Customers** is groups of people suffering from poverty or disaster. These people are the direct beneficiaries of Mercy Corps humanitarian services. The second set of **Customers** is individual donors and larger charitable organizations or foundations that contribute money, labor, or expertise to support Mercy Corps' humanitarian work.

What Jobs Do Customers Need to Have Done?

Mercy Corps' job on behalf of its primary Customer group is to alleviate suffering from poverty or natural disasters. Mercy Corps' job on behalf of its secondary Customer group is to provide ways to fulfill humanitarian and philanthropic duties and/or aspirations (as well as create tax deductions). In return for these opportunities, secondary **Customers** "pay" Mercy Corps in the form of gifts, grants, labor, expertise, or subscription-based contributions.

Here's a key point: **Any organization that provides a free service to one Customer group must also have another set of Customers who subsidize those who don't pay** (this is easily seen in social media or "platform" services such as Instagram, Google, or craigslist where the overwhelming majority of **Customers** use the service for free while a small portion pay for advertising or additional services).

So you can see that our two business model questions do apply to Mercy Corps—just as they do to any for-profit venture.

The Harsh Truth

What would happen to Mercy Corps if it stopped receiving donations and grants?

It would become unable to carry out its mission. Even if Mercy Corps' entire staff agreed to continue working without pay, the organization would be unable to cover other essential costs. Its only choice would be to shut down.

Every enterprise operating in a modern economy faces a harsh truth: **When cash runs out, the game's over.**

This is true for businesses, nonprofit organizations, governments, and nearly every enterprise operating in a modern economy.

Different enterprises have different purposes. But to survive and thrive, all must abide by the logic of earning a livelihood. All must have a viable business—or service—model.

The definition of "viable" is simple: **More cash must come in than goes out**. Or, at the very least, **as much cash must come in as goes out**.

You've learned the basics about business models— how Customers and cash sustain enterprises. But business models involve more than just cash and Customers. The Business Model Canvas, which describes how nine components of a business model fit together, is a powerful technique for "picturing" how organizations work.

Why Pictures?

Understanding how organizations work is no easy task. Large or complex organizations have so many components that it is tough to capture the big picture without visually depicting the enterprise in a simplified way. **The Business Model Canvas provides a visual shorthand for simplifying complex organizations.**

Pictures and diagrams also help turn unspoken assumptions into explicit information. And explicit information helps us think and communicate more effectively.

The Nine Building Blocks

The logic of how organizations provide Value to Customers[4]

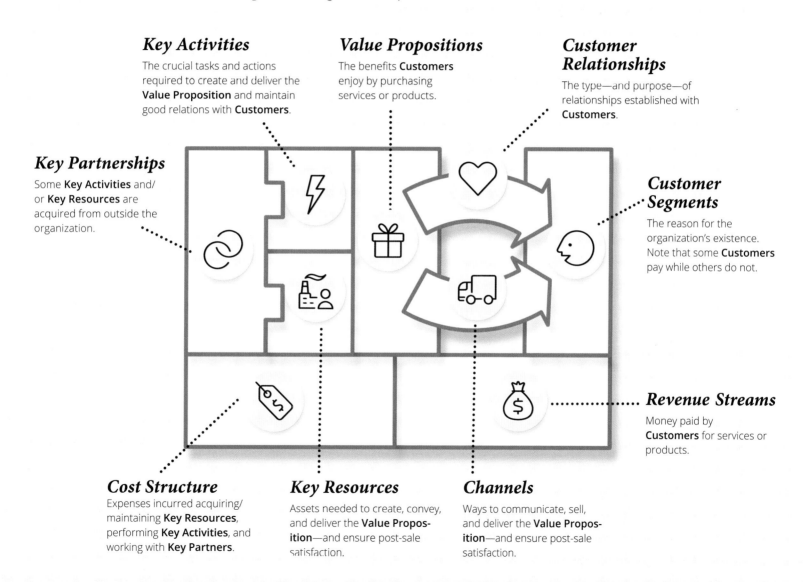

Key Activities

The crucial tasks and actions required to create and deliver the **Value Proposition** and maintain good relations with **Customers**.

Value Propositions

The benefits **Customers** enjoy by purchasing services or products.

Customer Relationships

The type—and purpose—of relationships established with **Customers**.

Key Partnerships

Some **Key Activities** and/or **Key Resources** are acquired from outside the organization.

Customer Segments

The reason for the organization's existence. Note that some **Customers** pay while others do not.

Revenue Streams

Money paid by **Customers** for services or products.

Cost Structure

Expenses incurred acquiring/maintaining **Key Resources**, performing **Key Activities**, and working with **Key Partners**.

Key Resources

Assets needed to create, convey, and deliver the **Value Proposition**—and ensure post-sale satisfaction.

Channels

Ways to communicate, sell, and deliver the **Value Proposition**—and ensure post-sale satisfaction.

The Business Model Canvas

Customer Segments

**Customers are the reason for an organization's existence.
No organization survives long without paying Customers.**

Every organization serves one or more distinct **Customer** groups.

Organizations that serve other organizations are known as business-to-business (b-to-b) enterprises. Organizations that serve consumers are known as business-to-consumer (b-to-c) enterprises.

As mentioned earlier, some organizations serve both paying and non-paying **Customers**. Most Google users, for example, pay Google nothing for its services. Yet without hundreds of millions of non-paying **Customers**, Google would have nothing to sell to advertisers or market researchers. Therefore, non-paying **Customers** may be essential to a business model's success.

Things to remember about **Customers**:
- Different **Customers** may require a different **Value Proposition**, **Channels**, or **Customer Relationships**
- Organizations often earn far more from one **Customers** group than from another
- Some **Customers** pay, others may not

Value Propositions

Think of the Value Proposition as Customer benefits created by "bundles" of services or products. The ability to provide exceptional Value is the reason why Customers select one organization over another.

Here are examples of different elements of **Value**:

Convenience

Saving **Customers** time or trouble is an important benefit. As mentioned earlier, Lyft offers a more convenient, trouble-free way to hail rides compared to traditional taxicabs.

Price

Obviously, **Customers** often choose a service because it saves them money. Zoom, for example, provides global video conferencing services at better prices than competitors. Zoom also offers free services subsidized by paying **Customers**.

Design

Many **Customers** are willing to pay for excellent product and/or service design. For example: Though more expensive than competitors, Apple computers, phones, and watches are beautifully designed, both as devices and as parts of an integrated application delivery system.

Brand or status

Some companies provide Value by helping their **Customers** feel distinguished or prestigious. One illustration: Women and men worldwide are willing to pay premium prices for Gucci fashions and luxury goods. That's because Gucci has shaped its brand to signify good taste, wealth, and appreciation of quality.

Cost reduction

Companies can help other enterprises reduce their costs and, as a result, increase earnings. For example, instead of buying and continuously updating their own computer servers, many companies now find it less costly to use third-party-managed remote servers such as those provided by Amazon Web Services.

Risk reduction

Business Customers are also eager to reduce risk, particularly investment-related risk. Companies like Gartner, for instance, sell research and advisory services to help other companies predict the potential benefits of spending additional money on workplace technology.

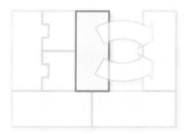

The Business Model Canvas

Channels

Channels perform five functions, which comprise the entire marketing process:

1. Create AWARENESS of services or products
2. Help potential **Customers** EVALUATE products or services
3. Enable **Customers** to PURCHASE
4. DELIVER Value to **Customers**
5. ENSURE post-purchase SATISFACTION through support

Organizations that own or control their own **Channels** enjoy stronger business models. Alternatively, an organization can engage a **Key Partner** to provide **Channels** as a Channel partner.

Typical **Channel** elements include: In-person or telephone; on-site or in-store; physical delivery; the Internet (web, videoconferencing, e-mail, social media, blogs, etc.); traditional media (postal mail, signage, television, radio, newspapers, etc.).

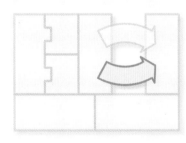

Customer Relationships

Organizations should clearly define the type of relationship Customers prefer. Personal? Automated or self-service? Single transaction or subscription?

What's more, organizations should clarify the primary purpose of Customer Relationships. Is it to acquire new Customers? Retain existing Customers? Or derive more Revenue from existing Customers?

This purpose might change over time. For example, in the early days of mobile communications, cell phone companies focused on acquiring Customers, using aggressive tactics such as offering free telephones. When the market matured, they changed their focus to retaining **Customers** and increasing average **Revenue** per **Customer**.

Here's another element to consider: More companies (like Amazon.com and YouTube) are co-creating products or services with **Customers**.

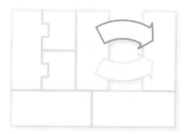

Revenue Streams

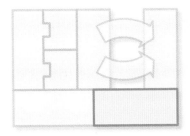

Organizations must 1) figure out what Value Customers are truly willing to pay for, and 2) accept payment in ways Customers prefer.

There are two basic types of **Revenue**: 1) one-time **Customers** payments, and 2) recurring payments for services, products, or post-purchase maintenance or support.

Here are different forms **Revenue** takes:

Outright sale

This means **Customers** purchase ownership rights to a physical product. Toyota, for example, sells cars that buyers are free to drive, resell, modify—or even destroy.

Lease or rent

Leasing means buying the temporary, exclusive right to use something for a fixed time, like a hotel room, apartment, or rental car. Those who rent or lease ("lessees") avoid paying the full costs of ownership, while owners ("lessors") enjoy recurring **Revenues**.

Service or usage fee

Electric utilities charge homeowners by the amount of electricity they use, and delivery services charge **Customers** by the package. Lawyers, doctors, consultants, and other service providers charge by the hour or by the procedure. Advertising sellers like Meta (formerly Facebook) charge by number of exposures or clickthroughs. Security services are paid to stand by and act only when an alarm sounds.

Subscription fees

News services, gyms, and online game providers sell continuous access to services in the form of subscription fees.

Licensing

Intellectual property holders can give **Customers** permission to use their protected property in exchange for licensing fees. Licensing is common in the media and technology industries.

Brokerage (matching or match-making) fees

Real estate brokers like Century 21 earn brokerage fees by matching buyers with sellers, while job search services like Monster.com earn fees by matching job seekers with employers.

Key Resources

There are four types:

Human

All enterprises need people, but some business models depend especially heavily on human resources. The Mayo Clinic, for example, requires doctors and researchers with world-leading medical knowledge. Similarly, pharmaceutical manufacturers like Roche need top-notch scientists and many skilled salespeople.

Physical

Real estate, equipment, and vehicles are crucial components of many business models. Amazon.com, for example, requires huge warehouses with massive conveyors and other expensive, specialized equipment.

Intellectual

Intellectual resources include intangibles such as brands, company-developed methods and systems, software, and patents or copyrights. Jiffy Lube® has a strong brand—as well as its own methods for serving **Customers**—that it licenses to franchisees. Telecommunications chipset designer Qualcomm built its business model around patented designs that earn licensing fees.

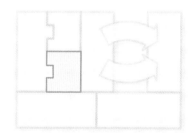

Financial

Financial resources include cash, lines of credit, or financial guarantees. Telecommunications equipment manufacturer Ericsson sometimes borrows from banks, then uses a portion of the proceeds to help **Customers** finance equipment purchases, ensuring that orders are placed with Ericsson rather than competitors.

Key Activities

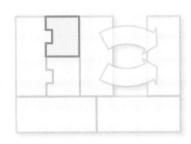

These essential actions enable an organization to create, communicate, deliver, and support Value Propositions by:

Making, which includes designing/developing/delivering services, solving problems, and manufacturing products. For service companies, "making" can mean both preparing to deliver services in the future and delivering those services. This is because services, such as getting a haircut, are "consumed" as they are delivered.

Selling, which means promoting, advertising, or educating potential **Customers** about **Value Propositions**. Specific actions might include educating or training, planning or executing advertisements or promotions, or making individual telephone or sales calls.

Supporting to ensure **Customer** satisfaction. Specific actions might include conducting surveys or interviews, then compiling and delivering results. Note that **Key Activities** typically exclude administrative tasks such as accounting that do NOT directly involve making, selling, or supporting **Value Propositions**.

We tend to think of our work in terms of tasks—**Key Activities**—rather than in terms of the **Value** those activities provide. But when **Customers** choose a company, they are more interested in the Value they will receive than in the task itself.

Key Partnerships

These organizations or individuals provide a Key Resource or perform a Key Activity.

It would be illogical for an organization to own every resource or perform every activity by itself. Some activities require expensive equipment or exceptional expertise. That is why securities and telecommunications firms often outsource their online payment security and fraud prevention activity to a company like Vesta that specializes in such work.

True partnerships go beyond mere supplier or financial relationships. For example, a wedding gown rental firm, a florist, and a photographer might share their **Customers** lists with each other at no cost to cooperatively execute promotional activities that benefit all three parties.

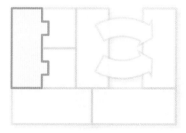

Cost Structure

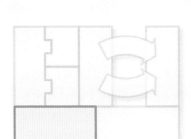

Acquiring Key Resources, performing Key Activities, and working with Key Partnerships all incur Costs.

Cash is needed to create and deliver **Value**, maintain **Customer Relationships**, and generate **Revenue**. **Costs** can be roughly calculated after defining **Key Resources**, **Key Activities**, and **Key Partners**. Employee salaries comprise the biggest **Cost** in most business models.

"Scalability" is an important concept related to both **Cost** and to a business model's overall effectiveness. Being scalable means a business can effectively deal with big increases in demand: in other words, it has the capacity to effectively serve many more **Customers** without straining or sacrificing quality. In financial terms, being scalable means the extra cost of serving each additional **Customer** declines rather than remaining constant or rising.

A mobile phone application company provides a good example of a scalable business. Once developed, an "app" can be reproduced and distributed at very low cost. The expense of serving an additional **Customer** who downloads an app, for instance, is close to zero. So whether the company sells three or 30,000 applications, its replication and distribution costs are almost the same.

In contrast, consulting businesses and personal service firms are rarely scalable. That's because each hour spent serving an additional **Customer** requires another hour of practitioner time—the extra cost of serving each additional **Customer** remains constant. From a purely financial viewpoint, therefore, scalable businesses are more attractive than non-scalable businesses.

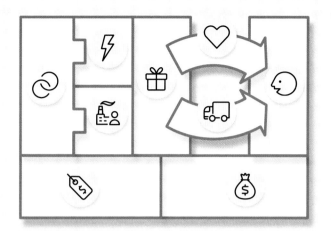

Together the nine building blocks
form a useful tool:
the Business Model Canvas.

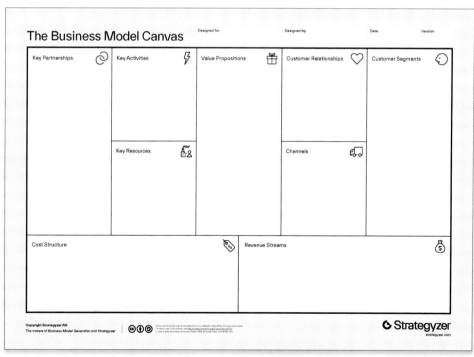

To download a PDF of the Business Model Canvas, **visit Strategyzer.com**

Now It's Your Turn

1. Draw or print a Canvas— or open a Canvas file on a computer or tablet

2. Place blank sticky notes in the Canvas building blocks

3. Write on the sticky notes to describe each building block

Now it's your turn. Try diagramming the business model of your employer (or your own business or main Customer) on the facing page. Keep it simple with these tips:

Write one item per sticky note. Don't use multiple bullet points on a single note! This keeps ideas separate and therefore movable.

Keep your **Canvas** simple and uncluttered when you diagram a business model for the first time. Once you have captured the logic at a high level, you can add detail.

Use precise language. For example, **Key Activities** should be verbs: write "Sell" rather than "Sales."

The Business Model Canvas

Designed for: Designed by: Date: Version:

Key Partnerships	Key Activities	Value Propositions	Customer Relationships	Customer Segments
	Key Resources		**Channels**	

Cost Structure	Revenue Streams

⬧ Strategyzer

strategyzer.com

To download a PDF of the Business Model Canvas, **visit Strategyzer.com**

Business Model Example: *craigslist.org*

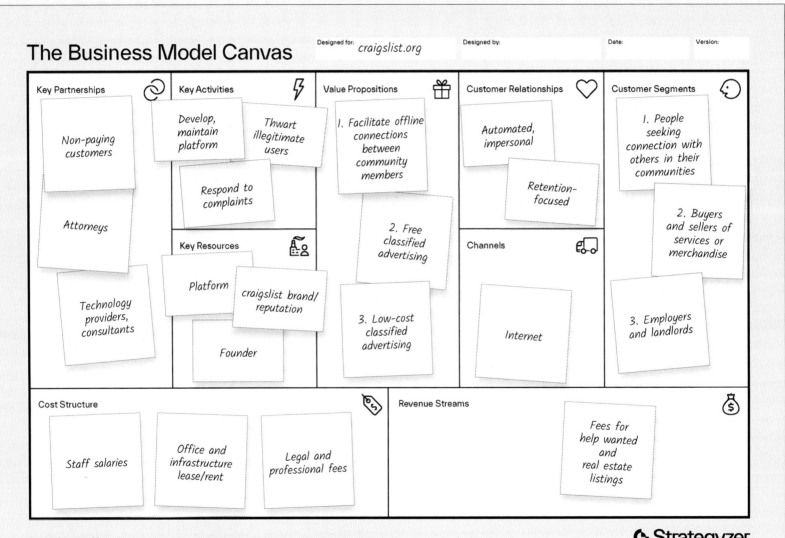

The Business Model Canvas

Designed for: craigslist.org

Designed by:

Date:

Version:

Key Partnerships

Non-paying customers

Attorneys

Technology providers, consultants

Key Activities

Develop, maintain platform

Thwart illegitimate users

Respond to complaints

Key Resources

Platform

craigslist brand/ reputation

Founder

Value Propositions

1. Facilitate offline connections between community members

2. Free classified advertising

3. Low-cost classified advertising

Customer Relationships

Automated, impersonal

Retention-focused

Channels

Internet

Customer Segments

1. People seeking connection with others in their communities

2. Buyers and sellers of services or merchandise

3. Employers and landlords

Cost Structure

Staff salaries

Office and infrastructure lease/rent

Legal and professional fees

Revenue Streams

Fees for help wanted and real estate listings

◆ Strategyzer

strategyzer.com

Craigslist.org, one of the world's most heavily used websites, offers classified announcements and advertising to help people connect with others in their community, find jobs and housing, and buy, sell, or barter services and merchandise. The company hosts 700 sites in 70 countries and posts more than one million job listings every month. Despite its non-corporate culture, craigslist is one of the world's most profitable firms on an earnings-per-employee basis: industry watchers estimate its staff of 50 generates annual revenues exceeding $600 million.

 ## Customer Segments

Most craigslist **Customers** pay nothing for the service. Instead, craigslist charges posting fees to employers and landlords in some cities. These paying **Customers** "subsidize" non-paying **Customers**.

 ## Value Proposition

Craigslist's main benefit is facilitating offline connections between community members. A second benefit it provides is free classified advertising, which **Customers** employ for nearly every service and product imaginable. Providing this free classified advertising service has generated a massive, devoted Customer base that lets craigslist offer a third benefit to employers and landlords: effective, low-cost job and real estate listings.

 ## Channels

Benefits are promoted, delivered, and maintained through the web, e-mail messages, and automated telephone calls.

 ## Customer Relationships

Craigslist users create, edit, and post listings on the site using an automated web and e-mail process that eliminates the need for intervention by craigslist staff. While craigslist relies in good part on users to identify scams, it also has a sophisticated user authentication/fraud prevention system based on automated telephone calls and e-mail messages. Craigslist concentrates on optimizing the user experience for current **Customers**: its basic design has remained unchanged for more than 20 years.

 ## Revenue Streams

Only employers and landlords generate **Revenue** for craigslist.

 ## Key Resources

Craigslist's most important tangible resource is its platform: the websites, code, databases, and server arrays that enable interactions between **Customers**. Its most important intangible resource is the craigslist brand, backed by craigslist founder Craig Newmark's reputation for public service and philanthropy.

 ## Key Activities

Craigslist's most important activity is developing and maintaining its platform. Think of it this way: Google could lose 100 engineers tomorrow without missing a beat, but having its website go down for a day would be a catastrophe. In relative terms, the same is true for craigslist. Most other staff time is spent dealing with fraud prevention and responding to reports of misuse.

Key Partnerships

Non-paying **Customers** are craigslist's most important Key Partners because they perform a **Key Activity**: reporting illegitimate use of the site. Note that the same group of people—in this case non-paying users—can simultaneously occupy two different building blocks in the same business model: in this case, both Customer and Key Partner building blocks.

 ## Cost Structure

As a privately held company, craigslist is not obligated to disclose **Revenues** or earnings. But it operates out of modest offices with a staff of only about 50, so its costs are tiny compared to other web giants such as Google and Twitter. Key recurring expenses include staff salaries, server and telecommunications infrastructure fees, and office rent. Due to its stature within the industry and the philanthropic programs it undertakes, craigslist also incurs substantial legal and professional fees.

A Way to Understand the World of Work

Maybe you are starting to see that the **Business Model Canvas** provides an extraordinarily useful tool for understanding why and how organizations function. The reason the **Canvas** is so useful is that it shows how organizations function as systems. The **Canvas's** power lies in depicting such systems in a simple, visual way.

Sadly, organization charts are often the only tool used to depict an organization. "Org charts" show structure and reporting relationships, but they do nothing to explain how actual work gets done and how the organization truly operates. The Business Model Canvas simplifies and explains the "white space" on the organization chart—the space where real work gets done.

"Simple" and "visual" are the keywords here, because most educated adults (including us!) are unable to grasp formal systems theory. And that's fine, because few of us use formal systems theory in our work.

But!

We can all benefit tremendously from basic **systems thinking**, which is simply a powerful approach to understanding why situations are the way they are, and how we can go about making them better. **The Canvas is a simple, useful way to understand any organization as a system**—whether that organization is your employer, a client, or your own venture. That is why *Business Model Generation,* the book that originally described the **Canvas,** has been published in 40 languages, sold millions of copies, and is used by hundreds of thousands of organizations and nearly every business school in the world.

But what, exactly, is a system?

Systems Thinking for the Rest of Us

A system is a group of interdependent parts that form a complex, unified whole with a specific purpose.

Not everything is part of a system. To be part of a system, there must be 1) a relationship or interaction between different elements, 2) an intentional design, and 3) a purpose.[5]

Pile

For example, a pile of bricks is simply a pile of bricks.

But when those bricks are skillfully arranged and joined with other related materials, they can form a system known as a wall. That wall might become part of an even larger system we call a house, whose other interrelated elements include doors, windows, gutters, plumbing, electrical wiring, insulation, and so forth.

A human being, too, is a complex system, whose interdependent parts include a heart, lungs, brain, muscle tissue, and countless other subsystems. All of these parts and subsystems function together to enable a person to survive, work, love, and play.

Beyond animate or inanimate objects, though, we can think of systems more broadly. For example, people waiting in line at a bus stop are not part of a city's transportation system—yet the moment they board a bus each of those people becomes an element of that transportation system.

A transportation system is, in fact, much like an organization that employs people and provides them with places to work. As with all systems, an organization has 1) a purpose,

2) an intentional design, and 3) interrelationships between different elements. And when we use the **Canvas** to model our employer, for example, we see—maybe for the first time—the greater purpose of the organization, the interdependency of its component parts, and perhaps most important of all, how we fit in.

Viewing a workplace as a system enables us to see our own work as an interdependent contribution to the organization's purpose rather than a narrowly defined collection of tasks performed independently of other people. It enables us to adopt what we call **Outward Focus**: one key to workplace satisfaction described on the next page.

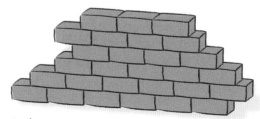

System

Thinking Ahead Is Good, Thinking Outward Is Better

As he walked through a warehouse full of unrigged boats and thousands of marine parts, Kyle Westminster's mind was swimming with to-do tasks and problems to solve on behalf of West Coast Sailing, the fast-growing seller of small and midsize sailboats where he had served as operations director for six years.

But Kyle groaned as he strode onto the company's truck bay and saw it littered with tools, empty cartons, wrapping plastic, and sailboat parts. *We have a delivery due any minute,* he thought. *They can't unload boats onto this mess.*

Kyle quickly located Alan, a recent hire who had used the truck bay to rig a new boat. The young man was beaming with pride that he had prepared the boat in time to be picked up by a new customer later that day, so Kyle was careful to first compliment him for contributing to customer satisfaction by thinking ahead. Then he gently explained that while creating customer satisfaction, Alan had also created a problem: blocking the truck bay just before a delivery was due. Alan had failed to see the bigger picture of how West Coast Sailing operated.

The two quickly set to work clearing the truck bay, and Kyle used the time to teach Alan how to practice **Outward Focus**, West Coast Sailing's systems thinking mantra for encouraging employees to see the bigger picture. Kyle differentiated it from "inward focus."

"Inward focus means concentrating only on completing your own tasks," he explained. "That's not a bad thing—it's just not enough. Outward focus means seeing beyond your own work to consider benefits to others who came earlier in the process—and those who will follow afterward."

Using the cardboard backing from a tiller package, Kyle sketched a simple diagram to show Alan how other people and activities at West Coast Sailing were affected by Alan's work that morning. In addition to rigging the boat properly so the customer would be satisfied—inward focus—he pointed out important **outward focus** considerations:

1. Check to see if and when a delivery would require Alan to evacuate the truck bay as his work area. Sailboat deliveries are a crucial operation that affect the entire company.

2. Return tools to the tool rack immediately so that others could use them, then clear the bay of any leftover parts and debris.

3. Record in the parts log everything removed from inventory so purchasing staff can re-order as needed.

4. Record in the vendor log the defective cleat Alan discovered while pulling parts for the rigging work. West Coast Sailing was a stickler for quality and carefully tracked supplier quality trends.

Kyle again expressed his appreciation for Alan's ability to focus on his own work and fulfill a customer's expectations. Then he spoke about the interdependent nature of all workplaces: how Alan's work was connected to—and had an impact on—other people and activities at West Coast Sailing. When the young man asked for a specific guidance on how to achieve outward focus, Kyle responded by saying that before undertaking any task, he asks himself two questions:

1. What can I do now to help the people who work before me and after me?
2. How can I assist with the processes that precede and follow my work?

Alan thanked his new mentor and moved on to other tasks. As Kyle headed toward the company showroom, his thoughts quickly returned to his unfinished task list, set back yet another 30 minutes by the unplanned tutoring of a promising new employee. *But that half-hour was well worth it,* he thought. *In the long run, Alan's understanding of outward focus will save us many, many hours.*

Though outward focus applies in every organization, directly helping customers can be so compelling that people tend to fall back on inward focus. That is why it is so effective to combine hands-on work guidelines such as Outward Focus with systems thinking tools like the **Business Model Canvas**. We are always amazed when employers orient new workers by showing organization charts, which simply depict structure and authority. Instead, why not also show business models, which impart clear operational understanding?

Now that you understand Outward Focus, let's move on to examine another powerful tool for understanding how non-commercial organizations work: the **Enterprise Service Model Canvas**.

We have learned that every modern organization has a **business model**, whether explicit or implicit, and that all must abide by the logic of earning a living.

An **Enterprise Service Model Canvas** uses exactly the same logic as the **Business Model Canvas**, but with language better harmonized with non-commercial work orientations.

For example, organizations operating in government, healthcare, education, and other non-commercial sectors often do not use financial earnings as the main measure of their success. As a result, professionals working in these organizations may be unfamiliar with business jargon such as "**Value Proposition**"—and in fact they may resist the profit motive implicit in the terms "**business**" and "**business model**." These professionals may prefer to use service models.

The Enterprise Service Model Canvas

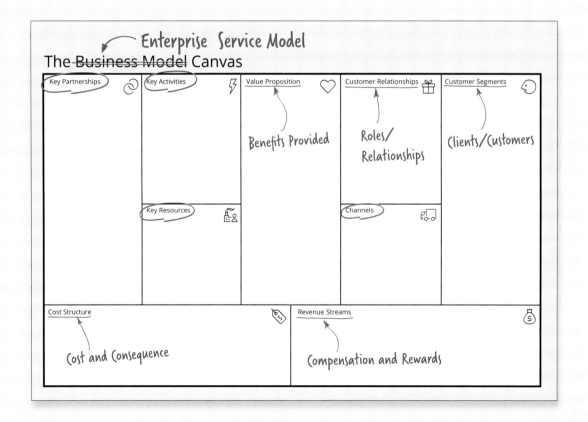

The Enterprise Service Model Canvas

Key Activities

Describes the actions most essential to creating and delivering Benefits, then following up with **Clients/Customers**.

Benefits Provided

Could include healthcare, education, security, food, clothing, shelter, or positive externalities such as citizen lifespan, better literacy rates, or reduced crime.

Roles/Relationships

Characterizes the role the organization plays—or the relationship it has—with each **Client** group. Examples include caregiver, guardian, educator, researcher, consultant, etc.

Key Partners

Describes outside organizations or individuals who perform **Key Activities** or provide **Key Resources** on behalf of the organization.

Clients/Customers

Clients are the reason an organization exists. Sometimes **Clients** are also **Key Partners**; the same entity can simultaneously occupy two building blocks.

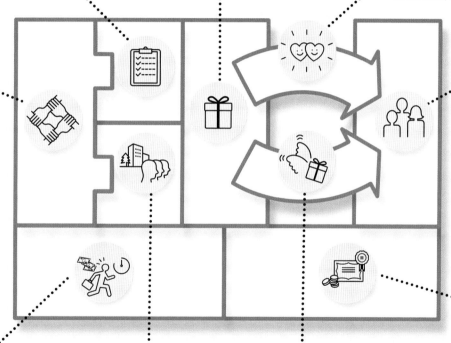

Compensation and Rewards

Tangible **Compensation** could include service fees, tax **Revenues**, grants, donations, etc. Intangible Rewards might include social contribution, recognition, sense of community, a reputation that attracts outstanding people, etc.

Costs and Consequences

Costs include salaries and benefits, building and/or equipment leases, professional fees, etc. **Consequences** might include adverse social impact, damaged reputation, or other negative externalities.[6]

Key Resources

Describes human, intellectual, physical, and financial Resources essential to communicating/creating/delivering **Benefits** and following up with **Clients/Customers**.

Channels

Describes how the organization communicates with and acquires **Clients**, delivers **Benefits**, then follows up to ensure **Client** satisfaction.

The Enterprise Service Model Canvas

Clients / Customers

Customers are the reason for an organization's existence, and no organization can survive long without paying **Customers**. But many non-commercial organizations do not use the term "**Customers**." Hospitals, for example, call the people they serve "patients" or "clients," while governments call them "taxpayers" or "citizens." So when you diagram the service model of an organization you are interested in, you might want to change the name of the **Customers** building block to something more appropriate for that organization.

Keep in mind that non-commercial organizations often have non-paying Clients or **Customers** who cost the organization money. Hospitals, for example, may be legally obligated to serve patients who are unable to pay. And governments may be obligated to serve, at significant expense, citizens who pay no taxes.

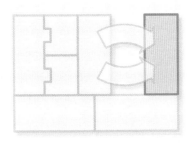

Some groups of people are important **Customers** of an organization—even though those groups may not consider themselves **Customers**. A public school, for instance, may treat its local community as a **Customers** because education helps create a more cohesive society, which benefits everyone, including people who have no children.

External **Customers** are the "end users" of an organization's service, like students in a school or patients in a hospital. Internal **Customers**, on the other hand, are coworkers or colleagues within the same organization. An accountant for a federal land use agency, for example, serves her agency's colleagues almost exclusively, and rarely interacts with private citizens (external **Customers**). It is worth noting that in medium-sized and large organizations, most employees serve internal rather than external **Customers**.

Benefits Provided

Like **Value Propositions** in a business model, **Benefits Provided** in a service model consist of intangible experiences. A return to wellness enabled by a healthcare provider, the higher earning power made possible by a university education, and a safe civic environment provided by government are all positive, beneficial end states rather than tangible things.

Avoid confusing **Key Activities** with Benefits! Remember: Benefits result from artful combinations of **Key Activities**—they are NOT the **Key Activities** themselves.

For example, the return to wellness described above (the **Benefit**) was enabled by diagnosis and treatment (**Key Activities**). Higher earning power (the **Benefit**) was enabled by teaching, feedback, and mentorship (**Key Activities**). And the safe civic environment (the **Benefit**) was enabled through policing and infrastructure maintenance (**Key Activities**).

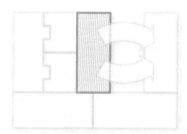

Finally, using the word "Benefits" instead of "Value" conveys a greater focus on the non-financial nature of relationships between service providers and **Customers**.

The Enterprise Service Model Canvas *Channels*

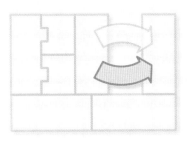

All organizations use **Channels** to acquire and serve **Customers**. But it is important to remember that **Channels** are a "two-way street." After acquiring and serving **Customers**, good organizations circle back to be sure **Customers** were satisfied with the service(s) provided—and make changes if **Customers** were dissatisfied.

In the healthcare sector, for example, most large providers use Press Ganey's survey services to get feedback from both patients and their own workers. Healthcare practices—and healthcare careers—rise and fall based on Press Ganey survey results.

Channels are sometimes taken for granted. But millions of service enterprises that rely on in-person, face-to-face contact saw their main Channel suddenly collapse when the COVID-19 epidemic struck in early 2020. Millions more had to adopt videoconferencing as their new primary Channel for conducting work both internally and with external **Customers**.

Roles / Relationships

The Enterprise Service Model Canvas

Like their commercial counterparts, non-commercial enterprises may play different roles or have different relationships with different **Clients**. For example, a hospital may play the role of caregiver with respect to patients but serve as a teaching laboratory with respect to medical students.

Similarly, a government welfare agency may serve impoverished citizens as a financial supporter but serve other government organizations as a source of policy recommendations.

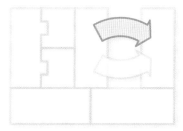

Compensation and Rewards

All modern organizations need money to continue operating. In commercial enterprises, though, financial earnings are usually the main measure of success. Non-commercial enterprises, on the other hand, often have non-financial measures of success. Governments, for example, may use average citizen lifespan or crime rates as success metrics. Public schools measure reading scores and graduation rates. Healthcare providers grade themselves on patient outcomes and other population health measures.

Non-financial **Compensation and Rewards** may accrue both to the organization and third parties who do not know they are being served by the organization, as when public schools help create a more cohesive society, benefiting an entire community. This is an example of a positive externality: a benefit enjoyed by people who did not choose to pay for it.

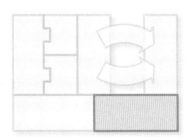

The opposite of a positive externality is a negative externality, such as air or water pollution: a cost affecting people who did not choose to incur that cost. Negative externalities are described under **Costs & Consequences**.

Key Resources

As with the other building blocks, there are few differences between commercial and non-commercial organizations with respect to **Key Resources**. When diagramming an organization's service model, keep in mind that **Key Resources** include only those assets that are crucial for creating and delivering Benefits to external **Customers**. For example, most organizations use computers, desks, and chairs, but those physical assets rarely contribute to the organization's **Benefits**. Similarly, most larger organizations employ bookkeepers and human resource managers, but these employees, while necessary, rarely deliver **Benefits** to external **Customers**.

Here is one way to decide whether or not an asset is a **Key Resource**. Ask yourself, Could this asset be acquired on the open market? If the asset is a brand, a reputation, a methodology, a patent, or a proprietary algorithm or database—in other words, something not readily available purchasable on the open market—it is likely a **Key Resource**. If it is simply a person, space, or physical asset that could be employed, leased, or purchased on the open market, it is less likely to be a **Key Resource**.

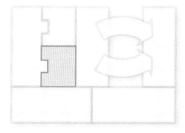

Key Activities

As with **Key Resources**, there are few differences between commercial and non-commercial organizations with respect to **Key Activities**. **Key Activities** include only those activities that are crucial for communicating, creating, delivering, and supporting **Benefits Provided** to external **Customers**.

Naturally, organizations must perform many actions in order to function: hiring, training, accounting, purchasing, logistics, and administrative tasks are all necessary. But these types of tasks are not **Key Activities** for most organizations.

One way to decide whether or not something is a **Key Activity** is to ask yourself, Does this activity directly involve attracting, acquiring, serving, or performing after-service for external **Customers**? If not, it is unlikely to be a **Key Activity**.

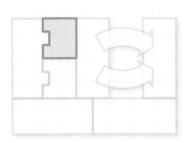

Key Partners

The Enterprise Service Model Canvas

Key Partners are people or other organizations who either 1) perform a **Key Activity**, or 2) provide a Key Resource to an organization.

Key Partners might include suppliers—but not all suppliers are necessarily **Key Partners**. For example, large government agencies purchase from thousands of suppliers, but many of those suppliers could be replaced by competitors that sell similar services or products.

When filling in the **Key Partner** building block in a business or service model, the key question to ask is, Does this party perform a **Key Activity** or provide a **Key Resource**? Or could it be readily replaced by another party? If the party could be readily replaced, it is likely a supplier rather than a **Key Partner**.

Here's another way to think about it: suppliers compete with each other to win organizations as **Customers**, but organizations compete with each other to attract **Key Partners**.

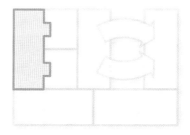

Costs and Consequences

All organizations, whether commercial or non-commercial, incur financial expenses. But non-commercial organizations may be more attuned to the non-financial **Costs & Consequences** of their operations. Negative externalities, for example, are described under **Costs & Consequences**. Examples of negative externalities include air or water pollution: costs that affect people who did not choose to incur those costs.

Organizations may suffer negative internal consequences, too. During the COVID epidemic, for example, many healthcare professionals experienced exhaustion or even moral despair due to unprecedented workloads and psychological stress.

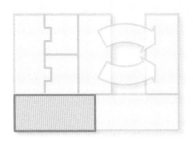

Finally, from a financial perspective, in the United States there is absolutely no difference between commercial and non-commercial organizations with the exception of tax treatment (non-profit organizations do not have to pay taxes on their earnings as long as those earnings are reinvested in the organization).

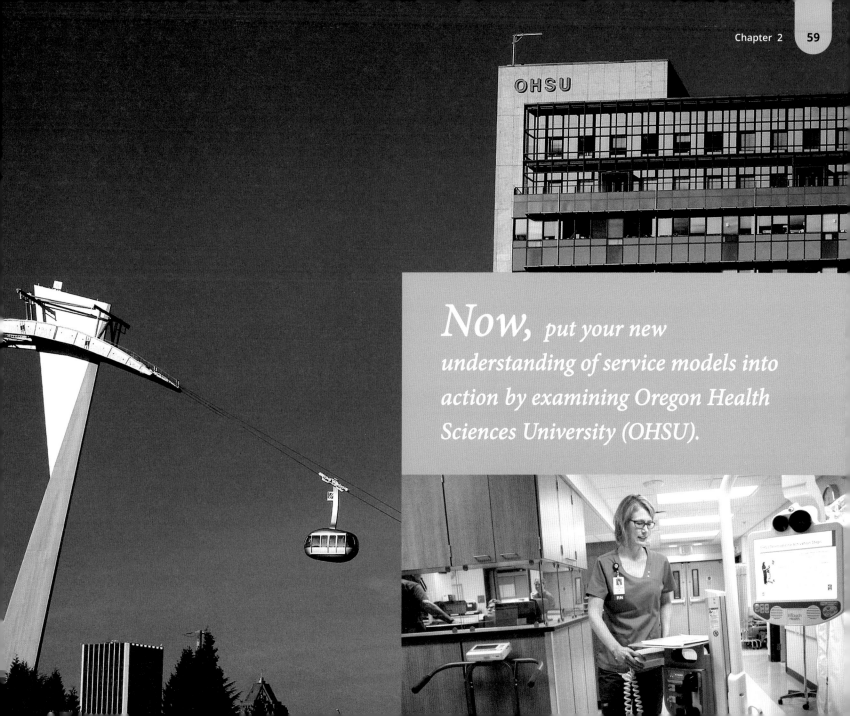

OHSU

Now, *put your new understanding of service models into action by examining Oregon Health Sciences University (OHSU).*

Enterprise Service Model Example: *Oregon Health Sciences University*

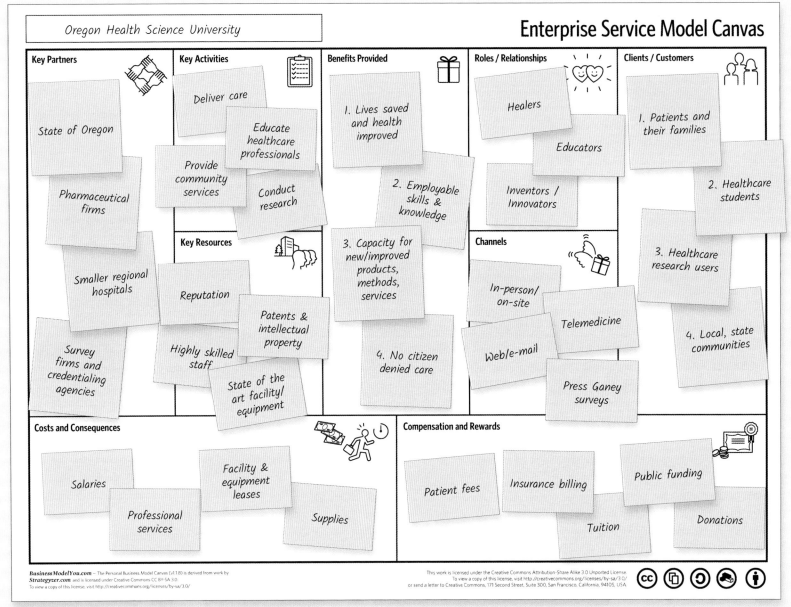

Oregon Health Science University

Enterprise Service Model Canvas

Key Partners

State of Oregon

Pharmaceutical firms

Smaller regional hospitals

Survey firms and credentialing agencies

Key Activities

Deliver care

Educate healthcare professionals

Provide community services

Conduct research

Key Resources

Reputation

Patents & intellectual property

Highly skilled staff

State of the art facility/equipment

Benefits Provided

1. Lives saved and health improved

2. Employable skills & knowledge

3. Capacity for new/improved products, methods, services

4. No citizen denied care

Roles / Relationships

Healers

Educators

Inventors / Innovators

Channels

In-person/on-site

Telemedicine

Web/e-mail

Press Ganey surveys

Clients / Customers

1. Patients and their families

2. Healthcare students

3. Healthcare research users

4. Local, state communities

Costs and Consequences

Salaries

Professional services

Facility & equipment leases

Supplies

Compensation and Rewards

Patient fees

Insurance billing

Public funding

Tuition

Donations

Oregon Health Sciences University (OHSU), Oregon State's only public academic health center, is a system of hospitals and clinics across Oregon and Southwestern Washington. Operating as an institution of higher learning with schools of medicine, nursing, pharmacy, dentistry, and public health, it comprises a network of campuses and clinical partners that deliver direct care to patients. OHSU is also a national research hub, with thousands of scientists developing lifesaving therapies and deeper understanding of diseases and their treatments. OHSU is a diverse service organization that employs more than 18,000 people.

Customers/Clients

The institution's complexity is reflected in the diversity of its **Customer/Client** segments. Note that the four **Customer** groups are ranked in priority order and numbered to correspond with a respective **Benefit Provided**. This illustrates the modeling principle that each **Customer** segment must correspond to a distinct and separate **Benefit Provided**.

Benefit Provided

Though OHSU is a medical institution, it provides more than life-saving direct care. Students expect educational and occupational value. State and local communities expect a public health partnership. And the pharmaceutical and medical technology industries rely on OHSU's research to enable

them to invent and innovate in commercial markets for drugs, devices, and therapies.

Channels

In the interest of improving healthcare for the greatest number of people, OHSU uses multiple **Channels** to create awareness and deliver services. Post-service feedback is obtained through surveys of employees, patients, and their families. Community feedback is gained through public hearings, electronic feedback, and institutional surveys conducted by **Key Partners**.

Roles/Relationships

Through its multiple roles as healer, educator, and researcher, OHSU maintains a complex web of collaborative relationships both within the institution and throughout the greater community. Client relationships vary from ongoing and deeply personal to automated and transactional, and include both short and long-term contracts.

Compensation and Rewards

Compensation sources vary from reliable to highly unpredictable. For example, the COVID pandemic prevented OHSU from practicing forms of service for which it was previously well compensated, while government research grants continued uninterrupted. Meanwhile, OHSU enjoys the satisfaction of contributing to statewide population health—and a stellar reputation won thereby.

Key Resources

Key Resources such as highly trained and specialized staff and leading-edge scientific and medical equipment make OHSU expensive to run. Compared to many other enterprises, both commercial and non-commercial, these resources are exceptionally difficult to acquire or replace.

Key Activities

Note that each of OHSU's **Key Activities** is matched to a respective Benefit Provided, which in turn is matched to a respective **Client** group. In other service organizations, some **Key Activities** may be common to more than one **Client** or Benefit Provided.

Key Partners

Partners include public, commercial, and not-for-profit institutions. Note that some pharmaceutical firms may be both **Key Partners** and **Customers**, illustrating the principle that the same person or organization can simultaneously occupy more than one building block in a model.

Costs and Consequences

Salaries are typically the largest cost in any organization, and OHSU is no exception. OHSU also incurs enormous facility and equipment costs, both fixed and variable. A rapidly aging population with growing healthcare needs drives all of these costs at a rate higher than inflation.

Next Steps for You

It's time to "behavioralize" what you have learned by turning it into action. Now that you have a "big picture" view of how organizations work, try diagramming the business or service model of an organization you are interested in. It could be your employer, a company you would like to work for, or a potential client.

1. Draw or print a Canvas — or open a Canvas file on a computer or tablet

2. Place blank sticky notes in the Canvas building blocks

3. Write on the sticky notes to describe each building block

Enterprise Service Model Canvas

Next, challenge yourself with the following questions:

1 Does the organization need to solve specific problems? Do you have the skills, desire, and experience to address these problems?

3 Any issues this organization needs to address? Issues are situations that need to be addressed BEFORE they become problems.

2 Do you have skills, knowledge, or connections the organization needs to better compete or fulfill its benefit promise?

4 What trends are affecting this organization? Can you help the organization capitalize on these trends?

Now, it's time to further "behavioralize" your knowledge by taking on the service model of a one-person enterprise with whom you are already familiar—you—the focus of the next chapter!

CHAPTER 3

Next, Diagram How You Work

The
Work
Model
Canvas

Canvas logic works for describing your personal work model just as it does for describing organizational business or service models. Note a couple of differences between the two, though:

- In organizations, the **Key Resource** building block can include a wide range of assets, such as brands, patents, proprietary methodologies, real estate, specialized equipment, and so forth. But in a work model, the most important **Key Resource** is you: your interests, skills and abilities, personality, plus any tangible or intangible assets you own or control.

- Traditional organizational business models depict only monetary costs and benefits. But work models consider unquantifiable "soft" costs or consequences (such as stress or inflexibility) and "soft" compensation and rewards (such as flexibility or professional development).

When drawing your own work model, you may find the building block descriptions on the opposite page helpful.

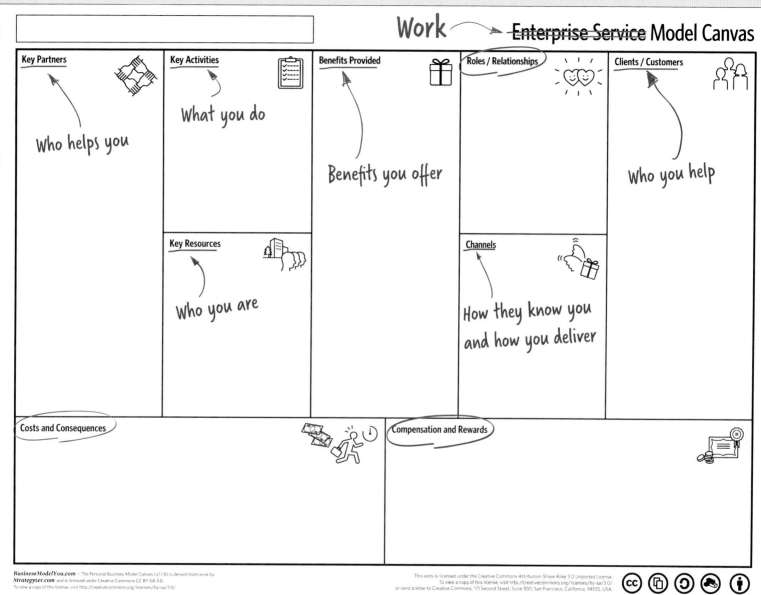

Work → ~~Enterprise Service~~ **Model Canvas**

Key Partners

Who helps you

Key Activities

What you do

Key Resources

Who you are

Benefits Provided

Benefits you offer

Roles / Relationships

Channels

How they know you
and how you deliver

Clients / Customers

Who you help

Costs and Consequences

Compensation and Rewards

Your First Work Model: Drafting Time!

This chapter is where your work model begins to take shape! So grab paper, marker, and sticky notes—or use a digital tool such as Mural, Miro, Google Jamboard, PowerPoint, or Keynote. You can download digital Work Model Canvas files by joining for free at Community.BusinessModelYou.com.

One thing to keep in mind: When creating your first work model, limit yourself to the professional work you do today to earn a living. Diagramming a clear, accurate picture of your as-is model lays a strong foundation for progress.

Here's the process we suggest:

1. Draw, print, or bring up a Work Model Canvas file onscreen
2. Apply sticky notes
3. Describe building block elements on the notes using the explanations and examples in the next pages as a guide

Start with any building block that appeals to you. If you already have a good grasp on **Customers** or **Channels**, for example, start with one of those blocks. Otherwise, we recommend you diagram in the order presented on the following pages.

The best way to diagram a model is to quickly "get some paint on the Canvas." Go with your first instincts; don't think too much. Avoid introspection. Rather than trying to get your model exactly "right" on the first try, it's best to make a quick draft, then modify later.

The whole point of using sticky notes is that you can easily move, change, or discard them. Take a design approach by iterating: starting over and redoing your model (again and again!). Avoid getting too attached to an initial idea. Starting over from scratch is usually faster and more productive than agonizing over what you already have. Let the sticky notes remind you that models must change!

Work Model Canvas

Who Helps You
(Key Partners)

Kamala

What You Do
(Key Activities)

Imani

Who You Are
(Key Resources)

Annabelle

Benefits You Offer
(Value Proposition)

Bernice

Roles and Relationships
(Customer Relationships)

How They Know You and How You Deliver
(Channels)

Elisa

Who You Help
(Customers)

Isabelle

These reinventors will help you with each building block

Costs and Consequences
(Costs)

Mark

Compensation and Rewards
(Revenue)

Jet

The Work Model Canvas

What You Do (Key Activities)

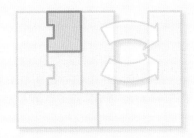

The easiest part of your model to define is What You Do—the most important activities you perform at work each day—so this is a good place to start.

Begin by describing activities that are the main reason you are paid for your work. On your Canvas, describe the truly important activities—the ones that distinguish your occupation from others—rather than every task you perform. Ignore administrative tasks. For example, most of us frequently read and respond to e-mail, text or wiki messages, or voicemail, but that is not the main reason we are paid. On the other hand, if you work as a customer service representative, responding to such messages may indeed be a Key Activity—the core reason you are paid.

Be brief and concise. Four or five words are plenty. One or two words are better.

Use verbs to describe **Key Activities**. If selling is a big part of your work, write **Sell** rather than **Sales** ("Sales" is a noun that sounds like selling is someone else's responsibility!). If developing software is a big part of your work, write **Develop software** rather than "software development" (use the plain short form of the verb rather than the noun form).

Your work may involve only two or three **Key Activities**, or it may require half a dozen or so. To start, you might find it helpful to simply list every activity you can think of, then delete the less important tasks as you work on your model.

THE ACCOUNTANT

Imani

What is truly important?

After earning her certified public accountant credential, Imani ignored friends' advice and took a job at an unglamorous manufacturer of precision metal components: a company with multibillion dollar sales and 30,000 employees.

When her new employee orientation focused on business models rather than organization charts, Imani knew she had chosen the right firm. At her three-month review, Rebecca, her boss, introduced Imani to work models. She asked Imani to diagram her own, starting with Key Activities.

These blue sticky notes show what Imani wrote:

- Check e-mail

- Import Excel data into SAP

- Run monthly exception report

- Attend meetings

- Update sales, expense forecasts

"Good start," said Rebecca. "If you had to choose just one of these as most important, which would it be?"

Imani thought for a moment. "Run the monthly exception report," she said, referring to a document that shows significant discrepancies between actual results and budgeted sales and expenses. "We aren't really paid to attend meetings and check e-mail!"

"Agreed," said Rebecca. "Now, think Outward Focus: Who uses exception reports, and how?"

Again, Imani thought for a moment. "The chief financial officer for our region," she said slowly. "I imagine he uses them to identify market risk or production problems."

"Good," said Rebecca. "So, I want you to add a new Key Activity to your model: 'Write callout report identifying and commenting on exception report discrepancies.'"

"I will," said Imani. "Maybe this means I can add a new sticky note under my Roles and Relationships: Risk Reducer!"

Who You Help (Customers)

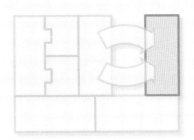

Next, add Who You Help—Customers—to your model. Recall that **Customers** are those who pay to receive a benefit (or who receive a benefit at no cost and are subsidized by paying **Customers**).

There are two kinds of **Customers**: **external Customers** outside your organization, and **internal Customers** inside your organization, such as supervisors, colleagues, or team members from other departments.

You likely deal directly with **external Customers** if you are self-employed or work in sales or customer service. But most people employed inside larger organizations deal mainly with **internal Customers**.

Your most important **Customer** is the organization you work for. So, write your organization name in the **Who You Help** building block. If you have a boss or supervisor who authorizes the organization to pay you, write their name in this block, too.

Next, think about who else depends on you—or benefits from your work. These people may not pay you directly, but your overall job performance—and the reason you continue to get paid—depends on how well you "serve" particular colleagues.

For example, if you are part of a computer or technology support team, you know all too well what it means to have internal **Customers**! Are there other individuals or groups within the organization you might consider **Customers**? How about key project leaders or team members? If so, jot down their name(s).

Next, think about other parties involved with your organization. Who purchases or uses your organization's services or products? Do you deal with them directly? Even if you don't, you might want to consider them your **Customers**.

Do you interact with any of your organization's **Key Partners**? Maybe they deserve a place on your **Customer** list. Finally, consider the greater communities served by your work. Such communities might include neighborhoods or cities, or groups of people bound by common commercial, professional, or social interests.

The Biggest Customer

Isabelle

With more than 20 years of diversified experience in different technology sectors, Isabelle is a seasoned professional who works at enterprise software maker SAP as a business development expert. She provides strategic and logistical support to salespeople who deal directly with current or prospective SAP Customers.

Over the years Isabelle grew interested in coaching salespeople at a personal as well as professional level, so she joined a work model training session.

Her first work model listed salespeople, solution developers, and several other internal colleagues in her Customer building block. After showing this as-is model to the facilitator, he asked a simple question that left her momentarily speechless.

"Who pays your salary?"

Isabelle recalled the moment with a smile. "When you work inside large organizations for years on end, sometimes you lose sight of the basics. I have to remember that SAP—my employer—is my first and most important Customer."

Benefits You Offer (Value Propositions)

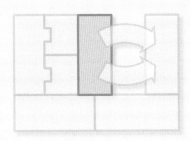

Now it's time to define the **Benefits** you provide to **Customers**: the positive experiences or end states **Customers** enjoy as a result of your work. As noted earlier, this is the most important concept for thinking about your career.

A good way to begin defining **Benefits You Offer** is to ask yourself: "What ongoing 'job' is the **Customer** 'hiring' me to do? What benefits do **Customers** receive as a result of me doing that job?"

For example, earlier we saw that the **Benefit** Kumon provides to **Customers** lies not in the physical act of providing instruction, but the advantages gained when students develop self-discipline and the ability to succeed in school. Parents "hire" Kumon to perform the job of helping their kids become more disciplined and academically successful.

Think of **Benefits** as a **beneficial end state or intangible experience** (disciplined and academically successful children) resulting from the combination of artfully configured **Key Resources** (Kumon's proprietary methodology) and well-executed **Key Activities** (instruction).

Again, note that Benefits differ from **Key Activities**. Understanding how **Key Activities** ultimately result in **Benefits** is a central challenge in defining or reinventing your work model.

Activity ≠ Benefit

Bernice

Bernice is a 38-year-old cardiac intensive care nurse who knows her job inside out. Every day she calmly handles medical events that would throw most people into a panic.

But in a recent conversation about the Benefits she delivers to people who choose her hospital, she drew a blank—until she attended a training session in work modeling.

"From the training I learned that patients perceive my benefit as reassurance rather than the clinical tasks that dominate my attention," she said. "When I thought about it, I realized no patient ever said to me, 'Bernice, I just love the way you monitor my arrhythmia,' or 'Bernice, you drew my blood so nicely.' But they often say, 'Bernice, you have been such a comfort to me and my family.'"

"Those comments about family stood out in my mind after we learned about outward focus," says Bernice. "It made me recognize that I am caring not only for the patient, but the patient's family."

Bernice is now taking a course in patient counseling and emotional intelligence. "I understand now that the things I say to patients might have an even bigger impact on their overall health than some of the clinical tasks I perform," she says.

When you can clearly define Who You Help and Benefits You Offer to Customers, you've completed much of the work needed to draw a work model. Now for the rest:

The Work Model Canvas

How They Know You and How You Deliver (Channels)

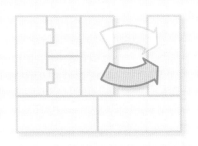

This building block encompasses five phases of what's known in business jargon as the marketing process. These five phases are best described in question form:

1. Awareness: How do potential **Customers** come to know about you?
2. Evaluation: How do they decide whether to buy your service?
3. Purchase: How do they buy it?
4. Delivery: How do you deliver what **Customers** buy?
5. After-service: How do you follow up to make sure **Customers** are happy?

Defining the **Channels** through which you *deliver* what **Customers** buy is straightforward: You might perform an in-person service; submit written reports; upload code to a development server; give a presentation; deliver merchandise, and so forth.

But as the five-phase process shows, there are other, more interesting—and more important—**Channel** phases, including **how potential Customers get to know you and the Benefits You Offer.**

Will they learn about you in person? Through word-of-mouth? From a presentation you deliver or an article you write? Via a wiki, website, or blog? Through cold or "warm" sales calls? Via e-mail messages or online forums? Advertisements? Through which **Channel** would prospective Customers prefer to hear about you?

Here's a common **Channels** problem faced by longtime employees of a single organization: they get stuck delivering to one internal **Customer** and neglect to develop awareness among other potential internal clients. Then, when markets shift or their employer reorganizes, they suddenly find themselves without internal **Customers**—or even out of a job.

Here's a helpful reminder as to why **Channels** are crucial to a work model: (1) You must *define* **Benefits** to communicate **Benefits**, (2) you must *communicate* **Benefits** to sell **Benefits**, and (3) you must *sell* **Benefits** in order to get paid for **Benefits**. You'll learn much more about how to communicate your **Benefits** and brand yourself starting on page 181.

Elisa

Changing Channels

Elisa's double major in biochemistry and psychology made her an ideal candidate for a biotechnology startup, where she started working as a product and quality trainer for new technical hires. She loved learning about new formulas and drugs, and her product knowledge was unquestioned. But after three years of rapid market growth, her workplace underwent a sudden and dramatic change.

Her employer was acquired by a medical device maker, which immediately more than doubled the number of employees. This created an acute need for leadership development, as the combined firm's greater size and complexity now required more formal management skills.

"I realized my training function was designed mainly for technical professionals," Elisa remembers. "Only the chemists and technicians knew about me."

Elisa recognized that she was invisible to a much larger and more diverse base of potential internal clients—especially new managers and their bosses. So, she revisited the Channels block in her work model.

"I had to deal with two Channel issues. First, awareness: How could I make new managers and their bosses aware of my training services? "Second, evaluation: How could I get those people to assess me and my capacity to provide training or access to other training resources? I needed an internal marketing campaign and different Channels if I was going to become known by new people who came in from the merger."

Elisa created an online product training course and an in-house training services website and newsletter, then took a bold step. She won permission to attend a new managers' meeting and deliver a short presentation about internal training services. That led to one new Customer who wanted product training for salespeople.

But the managers' meeting gave Elisa another valuable insight. "They asked some tough questions that made me rethink my Key Resources, too," she says. "I need to build my management training knowledge. I can't just geek out with the lab people anymore."

Roles and Relationships (Customer Relationships)

The **Roles and Relationships** building block characterizes the role(s) you play with respect to **Customers**. How would you define your role with respect to **Customers**? Are you a consultant? Supervisor? Expert? Healer? Researcher? Advisor? Counselor? Tester? Giving a descriptive name to a role you play helps clarify the **Benefit** you deliver to a particular **Customer**.

Keep in mind that you may play different roles when dealing with different **Customers**. What's more, those roles are defined, not just by you, but by **Customers** themselves. Some **Customers** may see you in an unflattering role—which is nonetheless important to include in your model!

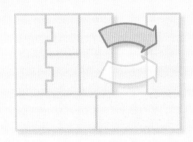

Think about roles in two ways: 1) they encompass socially expected patterns of behavior, and 2) they convey something important about your status within a team or organization.

It can also be helpful to describe the way you interact with **Customers**. Do you provide personal, face-to-face service? Or are your relationships more "hands off," relying primarily on e-mail or other remote communications? Are your relationships characterized by single transactions or by ongoing services? Do you focus on growing your **Customer** base (acquisition) or on satisfying existing **Customers** (retention)?

Different Customers, Different Roles

Bernice

Bernice, the nurse, described her insight about Benefits when she said, "Patients perceive my benefit as reassurance rather than the clinical tasks that dominate my attention."

Another change at the hospital caused Bernice to rethink Roles and Relationships as well.

"I always thought of my role as 'caregiver' whether the care was physical or psychological. But when my manager asked me to serve as swing shift floor supervisor for three months while a colleague was on maternity leave, my role changed completely.

"Suddenly I had a new Customer—the nurse manager—and a new role as 'supervisor.' I had to write the duty roster, check and submit paperwork, and manage other nurses, all while keeping some caregiving responsibilities. I didn't like it, but it made me understand that different Customers can require different Roles."

Bernice returned to her fulltime caregiving role just before the COVID pandemic struck.

"After COVID started I found myself smack in the middle of life-altering moments between patients and their families, trying to provide psychological reassurance," she says. "That meant I had to play different roles depending on what was happening. I served as therapist, spiritual guide, cheerleader, consoler, storyteller—you name it. Sometimes patients thought I was a jailer—or a liberator!"

That experience gave Bernice two additional insights.

"Having to constantly shift roles in response to patient and family needs made me pay more attention to nurturing my own resilience. When patients are angry or upset, it isn't with me—it's with the role I have to play for them. I'm thinking more about the Costs and Consequences of my work and starting to see my own therapist as more of a Key Partner than ever."

Who Helps You (Key Partners)

Your **Key Partners** are those who support you as a professional—and help you accomplish your work successfully. Key Partners provide **Key Resources** you need to successfully perform certain **Key Activities**—or they may themselves perform **Key Activities** that are essential to your model. They may also provide essential motivation, advice, or opportunities for growth.

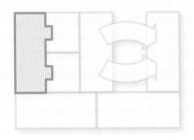

Key Partners can include workplace supervisors, colleagues or mentors, members of your professional network, family or friends, or professional advisers. Remember: the same person—such as your boss—can simultaneously occupy two different building blocks in your work model.

But pay attention to the word "Key" in **Key Partners**. Listing too many helpful people or organizations weakens the focus on truly critical elements of your model. List only parties essential for getting your work done. For example, if you run a production line, you're unlikely to describe the company's legal department as a **Key Partner**. But a supply chain manager might be crucial to delivering the **Benefits You Offer**.

List **Who Helps You** now. If you can't think of anyone who belongs in this building block, reach out for help: none of us can be successful completely on our own.

Customer as Partner

Kamala smiled with satisfaction. After more than two decades of hard work, she had finally been promoted to CEO of Digital Services, Inc., a provider of website design and management services to banks and private equity firms.

Kamala instinctively knew her new CEO role would require even greater outward focus, so she called on her human resources director, Roberto, who had recently trained in work modeling.

On a large Canvas pinned to a wall in Roberto's office, Kamala started to diagram her work model. Customers was easy; she quickly wrote "Digital Services, Inc.," "Banks," and "Private equity firms" on her first sticky notes. But when she came to Key Partners she hesitated as she pondered the role of a large client, Riverside Financial, in her new model.

Kamala recalled that Riverside had provided crucial bridge loans to Digital Services following the dotcom bust and the 2008 financial meltdown. Because of that lifesaving relationship, the firm had been given a representative seat on Digital's Board of Directors.

"Roberto, I'm confused. Riverside is essential for our financial needs—plus they're a trusted advisor on our Board. So, I was about to list them as a Key Partner. But they're already in my Customer building block. Then I thought they might be listed as a Key Resource, too. Which building block is right for Riverside Financial?"

Roberto smiled at this familiar dilemma. "Kamala, the same person or organization can simultaneously occupy multiple building blocks—and that's OK. Which two does Riverside clearly belong in?"

Kamala thought for a moment. "They are certainly a Customer because we serve them and they pay us. And clearly, they are also a Key Partner, because they provide financing, plus essential advice as a Board member." She frowned. "But I'm not sure about whether they are a Key Resource or not."

"Remember the definition of Key Partner," Roberto said. "Key Partners either perform a Key Activity or provide a Key Resource. Riverside provides you with a Key Resource, but they themselves are not a Key Resource within your model, because you do not own or control them."

A smile slowly spread across Kamala's face. "This model clarifies complex relationships."

Kamala

The Work Model Canvas

Compensation and Rewards (Revenue)

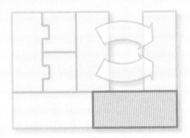

Describe "hard" **Compensation** such as salary, contractor or professional fees, stock options, royalties, and any other cash payments. Add "hard" benefits such as health insurance, retirement packages, childcare allowances, or tuition assistance.

Next, describe "soft" **Rewards**, including things such as professional development, flexible working hours or location, recognition, social contribution, satisfaction, enjoyment, or sense of workplace community. These "soft" rewards can sometimes be difficult to identify or describe. Yet many professionals have come to realize that so-called soft rewards are often more important than hard compensation.

For example, few people have a strong emotional reaction to getting paid each month: being paid is standard reassurance of adequate performance. Compare that to the reaction people might have to an announcement that their organization is relocating to a new city or state or requiring new minimum "in office" hours. The soft rewards of work-at-home flexibility, a brief commute, or high local quality of life can be high indeed.

And if you supervise others, it's more important than ever to realize that simply offering a cost-of-living salary increase is a weak incentive—and unlikely to be a decisive factor in retaining good people.

A Third Currency

Jet Barendregt served as an executive assistant to a senior partner at a European branch of accounting consultancy PricewaterhouseCoopers LLP (PwC). The work was demanding, and she commuted an hour or more each way. Still, "I got a kick out of getting things done and taking a load off other peoples' minds," Jet recalls.

As PwC's business grew, the firm added positions comparable to Jet's. But turnover was high, and Jet found herself coaching new recruits—even while taking on more responsibility. After ten years, Jet had become indispensable to the firm—but felt her hard-won knowledge and the value she provided were often taken for granted.

When her employer announced a location change that would dramatically lengthen her commute, Jet decided it was time to reinvent her work model.

She left PwC and set up a virtual personal assistant service whereby she served clients entirely through e-mail, telephone, Microsoft Teams, Zoom, and cloud-based tools. Her key innovation was in the Revenue and Benefits building block: She replaced her salary with a monthly subscription fee. Rather than being based on an hourly wage, her sliding fee reflected one of several support levels that Jet offered clients.

Within a year Jet eliminated commuting altogether, enjoyed more time for her children and other interests—while earning more than she did as a salaried employee. "People say there are two currencies in life: time and money," Jet says. "I believe there is a third: flexibility!"

Jet

The Work Model Canvas

Costs and Consequences (Costs)

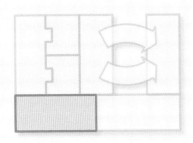

Costs are what you give to your work: time and energy, mostly. But **Costs** also include, among other things, stress or dissatisfaction brought on by disagreeable **Key Activities** you must perform, inability to use certain **Key Resources** that are important to you, excessive time or travel commitments, inflexible work hours or location, or lack of recognition or social contribution. What does it "cost" you to do the work you do? List the biggest ones in your work model.

Consequences in your work model can include declining health, low morale or psychological unease, disrupted personal or family relationships, or damaged personal reputation due to negative externalities created by your employer. Describe the biggest negative **Consequences** of doing the work you do. If not much comes to mind, talk with your partner or a housemate and ask them to describe what they see as the **Consequences** of the work you do. When we are too close to something, it can be difficult to see what others see.

You may also use your own cash or depreciating personal assets in your work, especially if you are self-employed. List significant unreimbursed hard costs. These might include:

- Workspace rental
- Communications, utilities, or transportation costs
- Training or subscription fees
- Commuting, travel, or socializing expenses
- Vehicles, tools, or special clothing

What Price Work?

Mark

"When Mark Degginger walked into my office, it was like neon signs were telling me that he had the wrong job," says career counselor Fran Moga. "He was miserable. He had a six-figure salary, a beautiful house on a hill, and a sweet boat in the bay. But he had to psych himself up to go to work each day. He took two-hour lunches and hit golf balls so he could tolerate going back to work in the afternoon.

"He worked for a very earnings-driven advertising agency; there was a lot of stress and internal politics. And he had health problems—a bad back. He was younger than me but looked older.

"The biggest problem was that he was competent, but work created a real conflict of values. He had all the trappings of success, but wanted something that would give him a sense of contributing to the greater good.

"So, one day I asked, 'Why do you keep doing this? Have you ever thought about what it's costing you?' He left without a word. But at the next session, he said, 'I understand now what you were saying. I'm paying a price in relationships, in health, in enjoyment of life.'

"When Mark arrived at one of our last meetings, before he even opened his mouth I knew things were better. He was more relaxed and his demeanor had changed: Everything was different.

'How are you?' I asked. 'Things are great!' said Mark.

"He'd resigned, and he and his wife had agreed to downsize. He had taken a position with a non-profit corporation that does training for disadvantaged and handicapped people. It was a big cut in salary. But he was so much happier."

The Work Model Canvas

Who You Are (Key Resources)

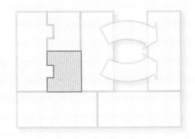

Organizations can attract and deploy significant intellectual, human, financial, and physical resources: patents, trademarks, and proprietary methodologies, highly trained specialists, cash, real estate, leading-edge equipment, and so forth. As individuals, though, we are "resource constrained"—we must rely primarily on ourselves. Your **Key Resources** include who you are: 1) your interests, 2) abilities and skills, and 3) personality, and what you have: knowledge, experience, personal and professional contacts, plus any tangible or intangible resources or assets you own or control.

Your interests—the things that excite you—may well be your most precious resource. That's because interests drive career satisfaction. One way to clarify your interests is to *describe what excites you most about your work.* Try this, then list your strongest interests in the **Who You Are** building block.

Abilities and skills are next. Abilities are natural, innate talents—things you do easily or effortlessly. List specifics such as spatial reasoning, strong empathy, or mechanical aptitude. Skills, on the other hand, are learned or acquired talents: things you've gotten better at through practice

and study. List specifics such as nursing, financial analysis, building construction, or computer programming.

Personality completes **Who You Are** (at least for now). Write down some descriptors, such as good emotional intelligence, industrious, outgoing, calm, poised, thoughtful, energetic, detail-oriented, etc.

Naturally, **Who You Are** encompasses more than interests, abilities and skills, and personality: It includes values, intellect, sense of humor, education, purpose, and much, much more. For now, though, let's move on to what you have. What you have includes both tangible and intangible assets. If you enjoy an extensive network of professional contacts, for example, jot down *extensive network.* Similarly, you might list deep industry experience, strong professional reputation, thought leadership in a specific field, or any publications or other intellectual property to your credit.

Finally, record any personally owned tangible assets that are essential or potentially useful to your work, such as a vehicle, tools, special clothing, money, or physical assets available to invest in your career, and so forth.

The Resource Is You

Annabelle

Dr. Annabelle Slingerland specializes in pediatric diabetes treatment and research—and is a strong believer in empowering young patients too often told that life is full of limitations and dangers. To promote her beliefs, Annabelle organized an all-volunteer relay marathon for children with diabetes. She dubbed the event "Kids Chain."

Shortly before the marathon, though, tragedy struck: Annabelle was involved in a serious bicycle accident. The Kids Chain event succeeded—attracting unexpectedly strong corporate, government, and media attention—but Annabelle became unable to continue her clinical practice as a physician. Her future seemed bleak.

Still, corporate and media interest in Kids Chain remained strong. "I didn't realize it was a potentially life-fulfilling project for me," she recalls. "I even tried to let go of it. But Kids Chain wouldn't let go of me."

A member of Community.Business ModelYou. com showed Annabelle how to use the Canvas to design a nonprofit organization that could support Kids Chain. Annabelle experienced a flash of insight while examining the Key Resources building block. "I realized I should consider myself one of Kids Chain's most important resources, and that the foundation should pay me for my input," she remembers. "I'd never thought of it like that before."

Annabelle created the nonprofit foundation Kids Chain for Diabetes and served as its first director.

The Power of "Third Objects" to Help You —and Others

People who seek professional career help are usually ready to disclose sensitive feelings and facts about themselves. And counselors or coaches are professionally trained to elicit sensitive feelings and facts and guide clients toward positive action.

But most of us do not seek professional help when we face career problems. Instead, we complain about our troubles to friends, family, co-workers, hairdressers, or bartenders. If we work for a progressive organization, we might confide in a trusted workplace colleague, supervisor, human resources person, or other thought partner.

Still, many of us have trouble accurately grasping and communicating our career-related concerns. Meanwhile, unless the person in whom we confide is a professional coach or counselor, they will have trouble eliciting those concerns, let alone providing us with effective guidance.

These situations call for tools that bring people together in a powerful shared experience, yet at the same time keep them comfortably apart, because they do not require professionally facilitated dialogue or direct answers to sensitive questions. A visual tool that participants can point to and treat as an object separate from themselves is ideal, as it appeals to people who are less verbal, more visually oriented, or who learn better through physical activity than through dialogue. Above all, these tools allow two or more people to focus on a neutral "third" object, freeing them from interactions consisting solely of words and dialogue.[7]

We call such tools "third objects." Third objects are tools that enable people to interact far more deeply, powerfully, and comfortably compared to using words and dialogue alone.

A work model is a particularly useful third object tool for career discussions because it offers a pre-made communication framework squarely focused on work, with clear boundaries and built-in graphical and language prompts. A work model relieves you and your thought partner of any worries about making overly personal observations or comments.

How to Use Work Models for Career Exploration

Here's an example of how you and your thought partner can use work models to facilitate a powerful career exploration session.

First, you might need to teach your partner work model basics, using what you have learned from this book.

Next, you and your partner should work separately to complete your own as-is work models, then arrange a place and time to share them in a "think out loud" session.

When your session starts, begin by asking your partner to decide which **Key Activity** in their model is the single most important one. Following their response, continue with "Say more about why that activity is most important." The idea is for both of you to focus on your partner's model—and to record your comments and insights there using sticky notes of a contrasting color. *Be sure to use sticky notes to convert comments and insights into permanent objects that can be reviewed*

later—otherwise you risk having these valuable thoughts vanish into thin air, as they too often do during words-only dialogues.

Next, you could look at the **Customers** building block and ask, "Which **Customer** is most important in your model?" or "Which activity supports your most important **Customer**?"

The key is for you and your partner to focus and comment on the graphical model itself—the third object—rather than the verbal dialogue.

You could then proceed through the rest of the model, building block by building block. Starting on page 130 you'll find more than 25 questions and prompts that will help you and your thought partner quickly arrive at powerful insights (keep in mind that third objects are helpful even if you work alone).

You may have noticed that **Who You Are and What You Have** is the final block in the model-building sequence we recommend. That's because it's easy to ruminate endlessly

on questions such as *Who am I? What is my career purpose? What do I want to accomplish in life?*

But such questions cannot be answered through introspection. They can only be answered, ultimately, through action, and over time—through lived experience. And diagramming your work model is a concrete action you can take now to objectively understand how you work—and prepare to identify "hotspots" and refine your professional identity.

Self-Check Your As-Is Model

1 Is your as-is model a fair representation of how you work today, or does it contain idealized content you wish was current reality?

2 Have you differentiated **Benefits** (an improved state or result, usually expressed with nouns) from **What You Do** (activities expressed with verbs)?

3 Different **Customers** must receive different **Benefits**: does each **Customer** in your model receive a different **Benefit**?

4 In **Costs and Consequences** and **Compensation and Rewards**, have you described only financial or "hard" items? Be sure to consider "soft" elements, too.

5 In **Roles and Relationships**, have you left out unflattering ones (such as when patients considered Bernice, the nurse, to be a "jailer")? Be sure to include unflattering roles.

In Chapter 4 you'll identify "hotspots" in your model, including painful roles you may want to change.

Reflect

CHAPTER 4

Now, Identify "Hotspots" and Refine Your Professional Identity

Now that you have diagrammed your as-is work model, it is time to reflect on the parts of the model that suit you—and the parts that need adapting.

Reflection—when properly done—can quickly resolve a surprising number of work- and career-related problems. But too many of us limit our reflection to self-reflection. The result is that the same unresolved questions swirl endlessly through our minds without leading to decisions and action. This is what we call "tornado thinking."

Time for Reflection

The cure for tornado thinking is to find a thought partner and "think out loud" together using structured exercises. We recommend inviting a trusted colleague, mentor, friend, or coach to collaborate with you as your thought partner.

As thought partners, spouses or significant others are usually a poor choice: they have already heard too many of your work-related complaints! And besides, they have a more important role in your life—love. You want someone who is professionally interested in—but emotionally detached from—your career progress.

So, seek out a promising thought partner. Maybe you can offer to teach them the modeling basics you have learned so far and help them diagram their own as-is work model. Once you each have an as-is model prepared, you are ready to take the first step: identifying hotspots.

"Hotspots": What They Are and How to Identify Them

Hotspots are pain points or unexploited opportunities in your work model. They are clues to elements in your model that need to change, so it is important to carefully identify in which specific building blocks they reside. Hotspots can be:

- Something that feels uncomfortable or that generates friction (for example, your main customer or client hold values that conflict with yours)

- An opportunity or resource that you have not yet taken advantage of (for example, external partners who could help you but whom you have not yet approached)

A vague sense of where work feels uncomfortable isn't enough. Diagramming your work model lets you see exactly where your hotspots are located. Then you and your thought partner can focus on them and take appropriate action.

The best way to understand hotspots and how to identify them is through an example. As you will see in the following case, analyzing a work model may involve observations and insights about things that happen outside the workplace.

Eric

Daughters and Fathers

Eric Seoh nervously patted the back of his head and twisted in his chair as he spoke to a career coach via Zoom.

"You're the first person I've talked with about this, other than my wife," he mumbled, looking down at his desktop.

The coach smiled, mentally noting the growing bald spot on the back of her 31-year-old client's head. "Let's review your model," she said, tapping her keyboard keys to share the digital whiteboard on which she and Eric had diagrammed his as-is work model.

The model showed that Eric served as a senior account manager for a large maker of electronic medical records software. His **Key Activity** was installing core software and database applications in large hospitals across the country. These installations were so critical that they had to be performed in person and on site, even amid the COVID epidemic. Eric had

proudly described the benefits he delivered as "better health outcomes." Yet he admitted to experiencing severe job-related stress.

"Stress is part of the price you pay for doing this important work," said the coach, pointing to the **Costs and Consequences** block of Eric's model. "Say more about the discomfort you experience."

Eric explained that because the software had to be installed on site, he traveled extensively for work. With some prompting, he admitted that his current role, which he had been performing for three years, required as much as fifty percent travel.

"Fifty percent!" His coach seemed genuinely surprised. "Anyone traveling that much would be under tremendous pressure. That's a lot of time to spend away from home…"

Eric's As-Is Work Model

| Eric | | | | **Work Model Canvas** |

Who Helps You
(Key Partners)

What You Do
(Key Activities)

Install software

Who You Are
(Key Resources)

Benefits You Offer
(Value Proposition)

Better health outcomes

Roles and Relationships
(Customer Relationships)

How They Know You and How You Deliver
(Channels)

On-site

Who You Help
(Customers)

Large hospitals

Costs and Consequences
(Costs)

Stress

Compensation and Rewards
(Revenue)

THE SYSTEMS ENGINEER

She noticed her client's eyes growing moist. "I sense that home is very important to you," she added softly.

"Yes." Eric replied slowly. "I have an 11-month-old daughter..." His eyes fell to the tabletop again.

"No wonder you're stressed!" the coach exclaimed. "Anyone would be!" She frowned for an instant, then took a moment to gather herself.

"Now, let's be precise about the location of your hotspot," she continued. "Almost everyone experiences stress as a result of working, so we have to look beyond the Costs and Consequences building block. We saw that extensive travel is essential to your model, so we could say the hotspot resides in What You Do. But let's go deeper."

She grabbed her mouse and drew a simple picture of a baby in the Who You Are building block. "My guess is that the real hotspot lies in Who You Are: extensive travel is simply incompatible with spending enough time with your family."

"Yes! That's exactly right!" Eric's face brightened. "But I'm not sure what to do about it."

"The first step is to recognize that you have entered a new life stage. Do you agree that your work must change to accommodate your family needs?"

Eric nodded vigorously.

"Good," said the coach with a smile. "Then all will be well. Let's take next steps during our session a week from today. In the meantime, I'd like you to think about reasonable ways to address this hotspot—things you might discuss with your boss."

Case Note:

Eric followed good reflection practice: instead of falling into tornado thinking or relying solely on his wife as a career confidante, he found a trusted thought partner who used a structured exercise to quickly identify the hotspot in his model.

Eric

Work Model Canvas

Who Helps You (Key Partners)	**What You Do** (Key Activities)	**Benefits You Offer** (Value Proposition)	**Roles and Relationships** (Customer Relationships)	**Who You Help** (Customers)

What You Do: Install software — Too much travel ✈

Benefits You Offer: Better health outcomes

Who You Help: Large hospitals

Who You Are (Key Resources): Young daughter home 🏠

How They Know You and How You Deliver (Channels): On-site

Costs and Consequences (Costs): Stress

Compensation and Rewards (Revenue)

Download the Work Model Canvas by joining for free at **Community.BusinessModelYou.com**

How to
Spot Pain
or Potential

There is no perfect or "correct" place to begin looking for hotspots. But the first and most valuable thing you can do with a thought partner is to simply present and explain your as-is models to each other until each of you clearly understands the other's model. This process alone is tremendously helpful: questions and comments force you to clarify your thinking—and modify elements to more accurately depict how you work.

Following that, it is a simple matter of picking any building block in the model that seems either painful or promising. Hint: Pain points are most common—and the easiest to spot!

Next, identify the single element within that block that feels most troublesome, and see if you can grasp the true source of the "heat" it is generating. As in Eric's case, you may need to trace this source to other, related building blocks.

As you trace the source, you may feel a renewed sense of how the building blocks interact and affect each other. For example, in Eric's case, the extensive travel described in his **What You Do** building block was a pain point because it negatively affected a more important element in his **Who You Are** building block: his relationship with his family.

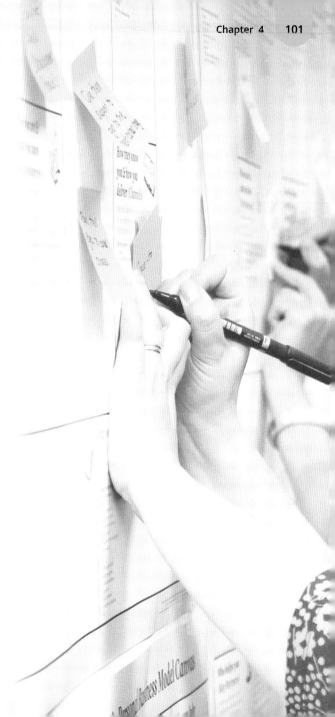

Try these steps:

- On your as-is work model, prepare sticky notes of a color different from the existing sticky notes.
- Write a brief description of one uncomfortable element in your model. Where does it hurt? Where is there friction?
- Place this note in the building block where you feel the discomfort. Repeat if you have more than one uncomfortable element.
- Trace the true source of this discomfort to other building blocks if necessary.
- Finally, shift your focus to promising elements. Are there people, skills, resources, or situations from which you could benefit?

A powerful way to deal with hotspots is to use The Three Questions.[8] Together these questions address every option available to you at any point in your working life:

1. **Is it time to Move Up?**
2. **Is it time to Move Out?**
3. **Is it time to Adapt Your Style?**

Let's examine what each question means.

Deal with Hotspots Using the Three Questions

1. **Is it time to** Move Up?

When you like your profession, your organization, and your role—and you want to progress—it may be time to **Move Up**. *Moving Up means progressing, not necessarily getting a promotion*. People define progress differently. For some, it may mean greater responsibility and higher compensation. For others, it may mean shifting into a more satisfying role, regardless of rank or compensation. For example, Kazue, a biologist, declined an offer to become a laboratory manager because she wanted to focus on conducting more complex research on her own. Keep on the lookout for employers that offer options for progressing besides simply becoming a manager.

2. **Is it time to Move Out?**

When there is no longer a good fit with your profession, organization, or role, it may be time to **Move Out**. Note that "moving out" can mean staying with the same organization but joining a different team, taking on a different role, or separating from a supervisory relationship that is no longer a good fit. For example, after years of proposal-writing, Victoria grew weary of the work and started thinking about leaving her organization. But after networking with colleagues, she realized her writing skills and service knowledge were ideal talents to transfer to her employer's marketing department. Note that forward-thinking leaders understand that discussing **Moving Out** options is not the same as questioning loyalty. True professionals and their leaders seek to find the best places or roles for people to exercise their talents.

3. **Is it time to** Adapt **Your Style?**

When you like your profession, your organization, and your role—but are falling short of the progress you want—it may be time to **Adapt Your Style**. Note two things: First, lack of progress may well be your own responsibility rather than someone else's fault. Second, competence is probably not the issue. Instead, it is likely there is something about the way you deliver Benefits that can be adapted to better fit your circumstances. For example, Stavros, a city engineering manager, realized from 360-degree feedback that he was overusing his project management skills instead of coaching his project managers to take full responsibility. Rather than moving to a better team, he needed to better manage his current team. Identifying and addressing a needed style change requires good feedback or coaching. When you need to **Adapt Your Style** but **Move Out** instead, you might simply relocate the problem rather than solve it.

Here's how Eric and his thought partner used The Three Questions to consider his options:

Together with his thought partner, here is how Eric answered each of The Three Questions—and made a decision:

Could Eric adapt his compliant demeanor to become more assertive and negotiate a travel schedule that assures he can spend Friday through Monday with his family every week?

Adapt Style

Eric's supervisor and colleagues were satisfied with his work results and style, so adapting style was irrelevant. More important, Eric realized that even regular long weekends with family could not satisfy his need for more family time. Finally, his thought partner pointed out that the hotspot did not reside in his style or in the workplace per se: Eric needed to attend to his personal needs for meaning and satisfaction.

Should Eric look for a new job with a different organization? Or should he stay with his current company but leave his account manager role and become an internal consultant to account managers who need remote support when they work at client sites?

Move Out

Aside from the excessive travel, Eric liked his work and his organization. His thought partner also cautioned him against quitting and looking for another job, explaining that quitting is often a simplistic solution that merely relocates the same "hotspot" to a different organization. On the other hand, **Moving Out** to a new role remotely supporting on-site account managers would require working odd hours and across different time zones, which would cut into Eric's family time.

Could Eric shift into a role teaching others to do the work he had mastered so well?

Move Up

As they thought out loud together, Eric and his thought partner realized that Eric's company needed to teach younger account managers with fewer family obligations how to do the on-site installation work—and that Eric was uniquely qualified to train these younger professionals. Eric decided to pitch his boss on moving into a training role. His proposal was accepted.

How to Navigate Career Space

The Three Questions can do far more than identify hotspots in your work model. They can serve as a powerful tool for navigating your lifelong career journey.

On page 16 we stated an uncomfortable truth about career journeys: most of us take on a more-or-less haphazard series of jobs that, over time and with luck, converge around a general theme. Our careers develop by default rather than by design. We call this hands-off approach to professional progress "spending your career getting one-job-in-a-row."

This one-job-in-a-row approach typically suffers from using the "launch and land" method of moving through career space. First, we "launch" a time-and-energy intensive search for work. When we finally "land" a job, we cling to it until dissatisfaction, boredom, or job insecurity demands a change. Then, we revise outdated CVs and revive sleeping networks to launch another time-and-energy intensive search to land another job.

Many people repeat this launch and land cycle again and again in the mistaken belief that it is a career strategy. It is not. **"Launch and land" is a tactic, not a strategy.** Most of us would prefer to rise above the launch and land, one-job-in-a-row approach to our careers. To do this, we need a bigger view of work—one that links our work models to the larger systems in which they operate.

These larger systems encompass entire bodies of work undertaken by many organizations, not merely collections of "jobs." For example, Eric was involved in the healthcare industry—almost an entire universe of work by itself. Specifically, he worked in the field of electronic patient medical records: a significant and fast-growing body of work.

Think of bodies of work as following laws of physics: what we might call the new physics of career management. Here are those laws applied to Eric's case:

1. Speed
Bodies of work move at a certain pace and develop at a certain rate

The electronic medical records sector was growing at breakneck speed and evolving quickly.

2. Momentum
Bodies of work are supported by history and market relevance

Electronic medical records have a decades-long history, but government regulations and the COVID pandemic dramatically increased its importance.

3. Direction
Bodies of work move either toward or away from your true nature as a professional

As a socially conscious IT professional, Eric finds the field of electronic medical records both meaningful and rewarding.

So, we see that bodies of work are in motion, traveling through the "space" they serve. They are not stationary objects immune to change. Because they are moving they have the capacity to impart speed, momentum, and direction to your career.

Having a career strategy means thinking ahead and staying aware of where you'd like work to propel you. It means keeping your "radar" on and scanning for other accessible bodies of work capable of moving you along your preferred career trajectory. And it means knowing when to use the speed, momentum, and direction you've gained from one body of work to leave for another.

Navigating the career universe becomes much easier when you link your work model to bodies of work rather than specific organ-

izations, because bodies of work endure while "jobs" come and go, like leaves on a tree. The key is to recognize that the speed, momentum, and direction of your work should be sending you somewhere, not keeping you somewhere.

The Three Questions will help you navigate the twists and turns of your career—and truly manage it—just as they helped Eric. Any time you sense the need for work-related change, get together with your thought partner, share your respective work models, and help each other with the Three Questions.

As you do, keep in mind the new physics of career management regarding **speed**, **momentum**, and **direction**. Of these three, **Direction** is the most challenging to grasp. So it is to **direction** that we now turn our attention.

Your "North Star" for a Lifelong Career Journey

Most people spend a lifetime striving to navigate an ongoing series of work-related challenges, opportunities, and setbacks. Wouldn't it be reassuring to have a personal "North Star" that constantly guides you in the best direction, no matter what twists and turns your career journey takes?

Well, you deserve a personal North Star—and this section will teach you how to create one. Your personal North Star is called professional identity.

Professional identity, like the real North Star, keeps you on track during your work-related travels. And like the real North Star, professional identity represents a direction, not a destination: you will never actually arrive at the North Star—yet it unfailingly guides you in the right direction. Professional identity will do the same.

What exactly is professional identity? It is the persistent occupational character that distinguishes you from other people who do similar work. While similar to personality, professional identity differs in that it represents your occupational essence rather than your psychological essence.

Rather than describing your personality traits, your professional identity describes how you work in ways that distinguish you from others—while satisfying and motivating you.

Think of professional identity as what remains when you are stripped of all job titles, college or university degrees, certificates, licenses, awards, or ranks. Professional identity transcends titles of any kind. Rather, it describes the benefits you consistently deliver and the style with which you deliver them to **Customers**. It concisely summarizes how others experience the **Benefits You Offer** through your work.

Your work model contains two building blocks that offer rich clues to your professional identity: **Role and Relationships** and **Benefits You Offer. Role and Relationships** can describe the way you deliver benefits to **Customers**. For example, Ani, a market researcher, is seen by clients as playing the role of "futurist" because she consistently provides them with views of what's coming next.

Similarly, the **Benefits You Offer** building block can describe how **Customers** experience the benefits you provide. For example, as one client put it, "Ani enables us to be proactive, not reactive."

In contrast, many professionals define themselves by over-focusing on skills and credentials that reside in the **Who You Are** and **What You Do** building blocks. While important, **Who You Are** and **What You Do** often describe things that most comparable professionals have in common—they describe the profession itself rather than characterizing you as an individual.

Younger or less experienced professionals often lack distinctive elements in their **Role and Relationships** and **Benefits You Offer** building blocks, so their models rely more on knowledge (from school or training) and skills and abilities, which reside in the **Who You Are** and **What You Do** building blocks.

If you are just starting out in your career, strive to be self-observant and take note of your workplace impact rather than merely your workplace activity. Relax—**you can and you will create a professional identity**.

Start with the superpower exercise described on the following pages.

Ellen

Define Your Superpower

A good way to begin crafting your professional identity is to define your occupational "superpower." Think of your occupational superpower as the means (and style) by which you accomplish work that satisfies other people. Others may do the same work that you do, but the style that characterizes your professional identity causes you to do it in a distinctive way.

For example, Ellen was a corporate communications professional who worked at Boeing. As the giant aircraft manufacturer went through yet another reorganization, Ellen felt her work assignments shifting in unsatisfactory ways. Did she need a vacation? A different boss? A completely different job? A new organization to work for?

These questions swirled constantly in her mind but were never resolved. Ellen had created a typical career "tornado"—too many unanswered questions and too little time spent selecting the right questions and coming up with answers, decisions, and actions.

Ellen sought the help of a career coach, who asked her to diagram her as-is work model and define its hotspots. She came up with two:

- In **Roles and Relationships**, Ellen wrote "**Writer (as defined by others)**"
- In **What You Do**, she wrote a single word: "Underutilized"

Her coach then asked Ellen to try describing her professional identity. Here is what she came up with:

- Strong writing, editing, and proofreading skills
- Strong ability to present concepts verbally
- Superior project management and time management skills
- A wide degree of creativity and latitude
- Strong knowledge and understanding of trends in digital media/social media
- Self-motivated with a positive and professional approach to management.

The coach gently explained to Ellen that she had listed things that most communications professionals could say about themselves—mainly knowledge, skills, and abilities that fit in the **What You Do** and **Who You Are** building blocks. The coach also shared his perception that Ellen's model failed to express a compelling but still-undefined professional identity—a perception supported by the two hotspots she had identified.

"Let's refine your professional identity," he suggested. Ellen agreed.

How to Define Your Professional Identity

"You define your professional identity by getting plenty of feedback from others," the coach began. "There is a reason why hair stylists do not cut their own hair and dentists do not fill their own cavities. Some things require an outside perspective if you want to get them right."

He added that being self-observant is difficult for most people—another reason they need to ask colleagues for feedback. Asking for such feedback can be stressful for those who have never done it, yet it is the single most important career action they can take. Creating a feedback-rich workplace environment, for themselves and colleagues, should be a professional responsibility on the part of leaders and senior employees, he explained.

"Ellen, you'll be pleasantly surprised at the observations others share about you and your working style," said the coach. "Let them know you are interested in their help as you strive to gain perspective on your professional identity. Schedule some time with a few colleagues and ask them to tell you what they experienced as special or unique about working with you, both in terms of results produced and your workstyle.

"As you talk with colleagues, take notes on how they describe you. Remember, this is not a list of activities you perform. **It is how people describe you based on the results you create**—and the style with which you create them."

The coach ended the session by giving Ellen a written assignment to complete before their next coaching session the following week.

Turn the page to read what it said.

Draft a Professional Identity

Interview three or more colleagues. Ask them to tell you what they experienced as special about working with you in terms of (1) results produced, and (2) your personal workstyle. Listen closely for statements containing these words:

— Results delivered
— Impact on others
— Satisfaction
— Roles (not titles)
— Abilities (not skills)
— Purpose
— Style
— Beliefs/values
— Interests

After compiling your interview notes, write a brief professional identity description (150 to 300 words). Remember, this is not an activities list: it is how people describe you (and distinguish you from other colleagues) based on (1) results you create, and (2) the style by which you create them. Feel free to include other sources of professional identity such as school, religion, parents, military, a music group, traumatic events, fun experiences, a mentor, genetics, and so forth.

The following week Ellen returned and handed her coach a single sheet of paper. This is what it said:

> My seasoned intuition lets me find the hidden stories in different parts of an organization that MUST be shared and understood.
>
> People feel a sense of pride and accomplishment when reading what I write about them. I am a corporate shuttle diplomat who can cross organizational borders into many functional territories and create strategic stories that make sense to colleagues in other territories.

The coach asked Ellen to read her professional identity statement aloud. When she finished, she looked at her coach with a satisfied smile.

"Now you are ready for the final exercise," said her coach. "Try to state your professional identity as a 'superpower' in ten or fewer words. Describe the end results you deliver, not the activities you perform."

Ellen set to work, and after ten minutes of drafting, wrote nine words on a pink sticky note.

> Intuitive diplomat who reveals and interprets others' proud stories

How Ellen Answered the Three Questions

With her professional identity clarified, Ellen used the Three Questions to decide what action to take. First, she recognized it was not time to move up at Boeing because she was uninterested in working in management. Second, internal clients were not suggesting that she adapt her style. They loved her work when she was assigned to the right projects.

Ellen decided it was time to move out of her current corporate headquarters job and join a Boeing division that had unique stories that needed sharing, both to change its self-image and raise its profile within the company. This division needed her as a shuttle diplomat to foster pride in its work and build new internal client relationships.

Carol

A Message to the Unsure

Robert Symons, a 55-year-old psychotherapist and London-based career counselor, smiled empathetically as Carol, a 37-year-old tax attorney, broke down sobbing.

Mr. Symons had just asked his client the trigger question: What had become of the spontaneous, excited child she must once have been?

Later, when interviewed about the scene, Mr. Symons noted he had seen it replayed countless times over the years.

What could be behind Carol's emotional response and the similar responses by so many others?

Mr. Symons attributed them to an underlying assumption, explaining that:

...the most common and unhelpful illusion plaguing those who came to see him was the idea that they ought somehow, in the normal course of events, to have intuited—long before they had finished their degrees, started families, bought houses, and risen to the top of law firms—what they should properly be doing with their lives.[9]

He went on to describe how his clients were "tormented by a residual notion of having through some error or stupidity on their part missed out on their true 'calling.'"

In other words, people believed they were meant to pursue a particular career path—one where they would both excel and feel satisfied—but had failed to find it.

Where do people get this idea?

The notion of "calling" originated in medieval times and referred to a sudden encounter with a heaven-sent command to devote oneself to Christian teachings. According to Symons, a non-religious version of this idea survived, and continues to trouble much of today's workforce. Symons's interviewer describes the notion as:

...prone to torture us with an expectation that the meaning of our lives might at some point be revealed to us in a ready-made and decisive form, which would in turn render us permanently immune to feelings of confusion, envy and regret.[10]

Many people feel that, even if they lack a true "calling," they are somehow not optimizing their work lives. How can they address such concerns?

As a professional career counselor, Mr. Symons points to a reassuring idea from the humanist psychologist Abraham Maslow:

It isn't normal to know what we want. It is a rare and difficult psychological achievement.

—Abraham Maslow

For many of us, it's a huge relief to learn that **not knowing what we want is normal, not exceptional.**

The "Passion" Myth

Are you "passionate" about your work?

Some lucky people are. But the truth is, most of us are not "passionate" about work.

Yet career books often say, "Find your passion and the money will follow," "Do what you love and you'll never work a day in your life," or simply "follow your passion."

Reading those sentences, readers must think, *I'm not passionate about my work. What's wrong with me?*

Well, if you aren't "passionate" about your work, that simply means you are normal.

There, don't you feel better already?

The "passion" cliches sound good but they're a myth. In fact, most people should avoid "passion" when selecting or changing an occupation.

The Myth of Pre-Existing Passion

The expression "find your passion" is based on the misplaced idea that people are born with a pre-existing passion that can be discovered through introspection.

Now, it's true that some people are passionate about some things from an early age. We see young genius musicians, artists, athletes, and so forth—lucky people who quickly developed true passion for certain activities.

But most of us are not born with a pre-existing passion, nor do we discover one in our youth.

This is for two reasons: First, passion develops over time, in step with experience and competence in a certain field—it's not something that pre-exists within us.

Second, insight about yourself, or self-knowledge, develops mainly through action, not introspection.

That's why few of us have a "passion" when we start our careers. First, there's no pre-existing passion within us. And second, we simply don't have enough experience and competence to develop a passion.

For example, Kelly really loves playing the guitar: he could play the guitar for hours every day. But if you heard Kelly play, you would say, "Well, that guy's an amateur guitar player with average skill."

Will other people pay to hear Kelly play the guitar? No. Will other people pay to have Kelly teach them guitar? No.

Therefore, Kelly's love of the guitar is not a good basis for an occupation. Why not? **Because he's not a good enough guitar player. You have to be highly competent at something in order for people to pay you**

to do it. Kelly's passion for the guitar does not create benefits for other people.

Here's another example: Carol used to have a real estate sales license, and during that time of her life she met a number of middle-aged couples excited about changing careers by quitting their corporate jobs and buying and running bed-and-breakfast properties.

The problem was that these people loved staying in bed-and-breakfast properties as guests. They saw bed-and-breakfast work as serving wine and socializing with customers, not cleaning toilets, changing bedsheets, and scrambling to re-book last-minute cancellations. They had little knowledge of and no competence in the bed-and-breakfast business. Becoming

bed-and-breakfast owners would be very risky for them **because they lacked competence in that area**.

This is why competence, rather than passion, is a better basis for selecting or changing an occupation. And in fact, competence is the foundation upon which passion builds over time. As you become more skilled in your occupation, you may very well develop a passion for it.

So Good They Can't Ignore You by Cal Newport is a terrific book that discusses these ideas in detail.[11]

Design Your Life

If you are unsure of your career direction you might benefit from the excellent *Designing Your New Work Life* book by Bill Burnett and Dave Evans.[12]

Like us, Bill and Dave take a design thinking approach to work. Here are some of their key points, recapped with permission.

Three Things You Can "Make"

In the world of commercial organizations, **money** is generally the measure of what people make. The more money they make, the more successful they are.

In the nonprofit world, **impact** is generally the measure of what people make ("making a difference" rather than making money). The more impact they have, the more successful they are.

In the world of creative pursuits such as art, music, and literature, **self-expression** is generally the measure of what people make.

The more their creative works appear in the world, the more successful they are.

So, if you do disaster relief for a nonprofit, expect to be rewarded mainly by the impact you make—and less with money or self-expression. Similarly, if you work for an investment bank, expect to be rewarded mainly with money, and less with impact or self-expression. Likewise, if you are an artist, expect to be rewarded mainly with self-expression rather than money or impact.

For example, an unhappy artist might confuse the value of her expression-making with moneymaking and make a false comparison: "I'm unhappy because I can't sell my paintings. I want my expression to have value in money."[13]

Or the nonprofit leader of a high-impact after-school program for low-income neighborhoods, keeping kids off the street and out of gangs, is unhappy because she wants to be paid like a software developer. She is confusing money-making with impact-making.[14]

The harsh truth is that in the modern workplace it is often difficult to have income-producing work also be meaning-producing work and/or a vehicle of self-expression.

The idea that the same work can simultaneously produce income, **impact**, and **self-expression** is a romantic notion that arose only during the late twentieth century. Until then, most people thought of work as an instrumental activity—in other words, something done principally for the sake of something else.[4] Most people, we suspect, derived more meaning, satisfaction,

and self-expression from family, religion, hobbies, or other non-work activities than they did from their professions. Maybe this is still true today.

All this is not to say that the three rewards of **money**, **impact**, and **self-expression** are mutually exclusive. Dave and Bill like to think of work as a "mix" of **money**, **impact**, and **expression** that can change with different jobs or at different life stages.

For example, some professionals find that early in their careers they focus on making money. As they mature, they become more interested in creating impact, and as they grow older, their attention turns to self-expression. Others follow a completely opposite pattern during their working lives.

Regardless of your life stage or occupation, though, take responsibility for your "maker mix" of expression, impact, and money—and the respective rewards. Pain comes from measuring your success with the wrong yardstick!

Aliana

Avoid
Gravity
Problems

Aliana was a professor at a university in Europe who was deeply frustrated by her school's refusal to accept her proposals for innovative new courses. During a group coaching session, one of her peers pointed out that she faced a "gravity problem."

"What's a gravity problem?" Aliana asked.

"It's a particularly nasty kind of problem that Evans and Burnett discuss in their book," her colleague replied. "They illustrate it with this story."

"I've got this big problem and I don't know what to do about it."

"Oh, wow, Aliana, what's the problem?"

"It's gravity."

"Gravity?"

"Yes, it's making me crazy! I'm feeling heavier and heavier. I can't get my bike up hills easily. It never leaves me. I don't know what to do about it. Can you help me?"[3]

The point is some situations are impossible for us to change and therefore are not actionable. These situations are called gravity problems.

Designers recognize that gravity problems are unsolvable and therefore unactionable. Designers only work on actionable problems.

Thanks to her colleague's feedback, Aliana recognized that trying to change the culture of a 130-year-old public institution was a waste of time. The only good response to her gravity problem—or any gravity problem—is acceptance. That means Aliana could either find another job or adapt her style by reframing the problem so it is actionable. For example, Aliana might reframe the problem as: **How can I shift to teaching the topics I enjoy—using the methods I enjoy—without proposing entirely new courses that require administrative approval?**

Remember we said that artists should expect to be rewarded mainly with self-expression rather than money or impact? Well, it may be unfair that artists are poorly compensated in this world, but to fix that problem you would somehow have to alter the entire market for art. You could try doing that, but we would recommend that you accept it as an unactionable situation—a gravity problem—and instead turn your attention to an actionable problem.[15]

Recognizing a gravity problem—a situation that is impossible for you to change—may require a combination of outward focus, experience, or a third-party perspective, as in Aliana's case.

Remember that it is impossible to fight reality: water does not flow uphill, and fish do not live in trees. As you move ahead with reinventing how you work, **recognize and avoid trying to solve gravity problems.**

Stuck? Try This

If you are successfully avoiding gravity problems and are clear-eyed about the "mix" of rewards you seek from work—but still feel stuck or sense a need to reinvent your work from scratch—try this exercise.

The Lifeline Discovery

Most career coaches agree that work satisfaction is driven, among other things, by three factors: interests, skills and abilities, and personality. Where these three factors converge is your career "sweet spot." The Lifeline Discovery exercise helps you define and see where these factors converge in your own life: all in a fun, indirect, visual way. Here is how to do it.

a. Find a Partner

We recommend doing this exercise with a thought partner who is also interested in career development (see thought partner suggestions in Chapter 10). While doing the exercise alone is helpful, you'll learn far more by working with another person.

b. Time, Place, and Tools

All you need is paper and pencil for taking notes, some markers, tape, and a blank Lifeline like the one below (or the digital equivalent of all of these). It's best to draw your own Lifeline on a bigger sheet of paper—the bigger the better. Schedule a quiet time and place with your partner and be prepared to spend at least one hour doing the exercise together. Each of you will draw your own separate Lifeline.

c. Plot the High and Low Points of Your Life on the Lifeline

Tape your Lifelines to separate walls. Note that the horizontal axis of the Lifeline represents time, and the vertical axis represents enjoyment and/or excitement. Now, stretching back as far as you can remember, recall events representing high (+) and low (-) points in your life and plot them on your Lifeline. Jot them down quickly as they come to mind: let emotional rather than intellectual memory bring forth your high and low points.

Excitement / Enjoyment

My Lifeline

"High points" and "low points" mean:

- Specific, important events in your life: good or bad, personal or professional—whether related to work, social life, love, hobbies, academics, spiritual pursuits, or other areas
- Milestones or landmarks you remember clearly and are associated with strong feelings

- Changes in your career, both positive and negative

For now, plot each event on your Lifeline with a point and a short text description, such as "married Jan," "Mom died," or "got job at Vesta." Start at the far left with the earliest

high or low point you can remember, and then work toward the present. When you have plotted a dozen or so events, draw a line connecting each of the points.

Your Lifeline may now look something like Darcy's below.

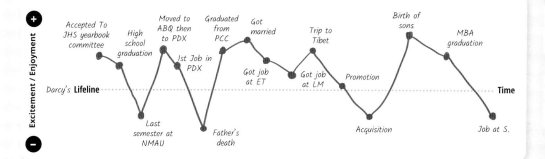

Darcy

d. Describe the Events

On your note paper, write a concise sentence or two describing each event. Use action words, such as "designed," "led," or "assembled." Try to describe each event using two or more verbs. For example, if you delivered a solo rendition of a song at a junior high school assembly, rather than "sang song," write "selected, rehearsed, and performed 'Achy Breaky Heart' at schoolwide talent show. Drew big applause!"

As part of this step, include the context in which you acted—in other words, write down the place and theme of the event. In the example above, the context is "schoolwide talent show."

e. Peer Coach to Gain Insight

Now it is time for you and your partner to uncover insights from your work. Act as a "secretary" for your partner by recording their responses as you ask the following questions about their Lifeline:

1. What do the high points on your Lifeline have in common? (Probe to see if your partner can identify common activities, themes, contexts, or people in their high points.)

2. How did you feel about yourself at each high point? Why?

3. What do the low points on your Lifeline have in common? (Probe to see if your partner can identify common activities, themes, contexts, or people in their low points.)

4. How did you feel about yourself at each low point? Why?

5. For which work transitions did you make the key decision regarding the change? Were these mostly career highs or career lows? (Career coaches agree that an internal locus of control is crucial to career satisfaction. Internal locus of control means you decide for yourself what you want to do, rather than being influenced by external parties: family, friends, colleagues, society at large.)

Switch roles and have your partner coach you and take notes.

f. Share Notes with Your Partner

Share with your partner the notes you made while coaching them. Be sure to use the same words you heard them say—but see if you can suggest some connections, commonalities, or emotional reactions they may have missed.

Then, switch roles and have your partner share what they heard you say about your Lifeline.

With some additional reflection and conversation, both of you should come to a newfound appreciation of where interests, skills/abilities, and personality can intersect to form new career "sweet spots."

Are you ready to revise your work model?

Before Turning the Page, Ask Yourself:

1 Is self-reflection getting me enough insight? Here are two people I might invite to be think out loud partners:

1.

2.

2 Are the hotspots in my work model mostly pain or potential?

3 If the hotspots are pain points, are they gravity problems I can't influence? If so, should I move out of my current role, team, organization, or even profession?

4 If the hotspots are unleveraged opportunities, what thoughts or beliefs keep me from acting on them? Should I focus on development rather than an exit strategy?

5 Can I describe my professional identity to another person? Which colleagues could give me good feedback on how others perceive the Benefits I deliver at work?

In Chapter 5 **you'll learn how to revise your work model—and whether you should be employed or start your own venture.**

CHAPTER 5

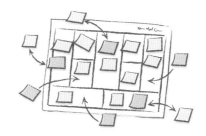

Revise Your Work Model

A New Role for a New Customer

Eric Seoh fidgeted in the chair outside his supervisor's office. He was early for his appointment and even more nervous than usual given that he was about to propose a career-altering shift in his work at EPIC.

Together with his coach, Eric had identified a critical hotspot in his as-is model: His role as a father was incompatible with the extensive travel his work required (page 96).

As Eric and his coach sketched out a new to-be model that could overcome the hotspot problem—yet remain compatible with Eric's skills, abilities, and interests—they identified a promising new workplace role for Eric: training junior system engineers to manage on-site software installation and upgrades. The training role would eliminate travel on Eric's part while creating a new pool of younger, installation-qualified systems engineers, most of whom had few family obligations and were willing to travel for work.

Eric

As he waited for his supervisor, Eric's thoughts turned to the three building blocks that had changed in his to-be work model.

First, he would have a new internal client group: junior system engineers. Until now, his three main clients had been EPIC, his supervisor, and IT managers at large hospitals, but Eric was confident he could serve younger systems engineers. After all, he was an expert in their shared world of software and information technology.

Second, his role would shift from "installation expert" to "technical trainer." Though Eric was less certain about this change in role, he had confidence in his technical skills, product knowledge, and installation experience.

The third change was in his Benefits Offered building block. Eric would offer EPIC the benefit of "retaining outstanding employees" by providing junior systems engineers with internal growth opportunities via training—opportunities that would encourage them to stay with the company. Still, Eric worried that his supervisor might perceive his new model merely as a solution to his personal dilemma rather than as a true benefit to EPIC.

"Eric? Sorry for the delay..." His supervisor's voice broke into Eric's thoughts. He drew a deep breath and stepped into her office.

How are you feeling at this point?

Maybe you experienced an important insight when you diagrammed your as-is work model, then made an adjustment—and now are reading this chapter simply out of curiosity. That frequently happens!

Or maybe you would like to go deeper and take a more studied approach to revising your model. If that's the case, this chapter presents a simple, step-by-step way to do just that.

How to Revise Your Work Model

Step 1. Re-Diagram Your As-Is Model

Diagram your as-is once again on the opposite page, or on a separate Canvas—the bigger the better. This time, guided by refined professional identity and other insights from previous chapters, you should be able to more powerfully articulate Benefits You Offer, Who You Help, and What You Do.

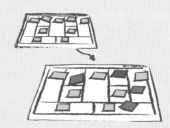

Step 2. Identify Hotspots

Where does work feel uncomfortable or as if opportunities are being missed? Circle building blocks on your model where you sense these "hotspots." For example, if you want to make more money, circle the Compensation and Rewards block. Or if you dislike selling—yet that's one of your most important activities—circle the What You Do block.

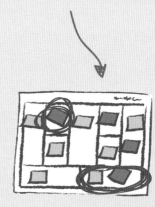

Work Model Canvas

Who Helps You (Key Partners)	What You Do (Key Activities)	Benefits You Offer (Value Proposition)	Roles and Relationships (Customer Relationships)	Who You Help (Customers)

Who You Are (Key Resources)

How They Know You and How You Deliver (Channels)

Costs and Consequences (Costs)

Compensation and Rewards (Revenue)

Step 3. Ask Diagnostic Questions

Next, answer the questions about your hotspot building block(s) on the following pages. Some questions deal with problems; others address opportunities. Either way, look under "Solution Starting Points" for hints about actions to consider. This section addresses both employed and self-employed professionals (more about self-employment on page 146).

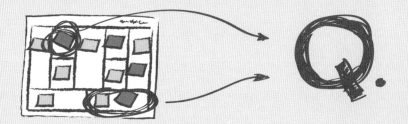

What You Do and Who You Are

Questions and Solution Starting Points

> **Are you interested in your work?**

If so, great—now go deeper and describe specifically what you find exciting about your work. If you're uninterested in your work, there's a mismatch between **Who You Are** and **What You Do**. Try the Lifeline Discovery (page 120) or Draft a Professional Identity (page 110) exercises, preferably with thought partners.

> **Are you underutilizing or not using an important ability or skill?**

A missing or underused ability or skill can cause stress or dissatisfaction. Can you add that ability or skill to **What You Do** in a way that supports or improves **Benefits You Offer**?

> **Do your interests and personality match your workplace? (Remember, "workplace" is largely defined by the people you work with). Do your interests and personality harmonize with your activities?**

If so, great! If not, can you add to or modify **What You Do**—or work with more compatible **Customers** or **Partners**? **Customers** are closely linked to **Benefits You Offer**, so check **Benefits You Offer** diagnosis questions (page 132).

Who You Help
Questions and Solution Starting Points

Do you enjoy the organization(s) or people you serve?

If so, great—now go deeper and say more about what you like. If you don't enjoy your clients—whether they are internal or external—can you find new ones within your organization, or within the same industry sector? If not, start over from scratch.

Who is your most important client or customer?

Do you and your client(s) agree on the benefit(s) you provide to them? Are you properly valuing the benefit you provide? Do your clients deserve a new or updated benefit?

Is serving your clients or customers too "costly"?

Are hard or soft costs too high to justify serving **Who You Help**? Are **Compensation and Rewards** too low? If so, work through **Benefits You Offer**, **Costs and Consequences**, and **Compensation and Rewards** diagnosis questions, or identify other potential customers or clients.

What is the real job your customer wants to get done? Do they have a "bigger picture" reason for engaging your services? For example, does your customer serve another, larger customer who has a bigger Job-to-be-done?

Clarify whether your clients are customers or consumers. Children are **consumers** of ice cream, but parents are the **customers** who pay for the ice cream. If your clients are consumers, are you effectively presenting the **Benefits You Offer** to the paying **Customer**? Can you reconceive, reposition, or modify the **Benefits You Offer** to help customers succeed with bigger or more valuable jobs?

Do customers equate What You Do with their Job-to-be-done? Do you?

Sometimes customers themselves haven't clearly defined jobs-to-be-done. Can you assist with this definition? Can you redefine or modify **What You Do** to boost **Benefits You Offer**?

Do you need new customers?

If so, consider changing your focus from customer retention to customer acquisition. Do you need to do more selling or marketing? Improve or develop your skills in this area? Find partners who can help you acquire new customers?

Benefits You Offer
Questions and Solution Starting Points

What elements of your services are truly valued by customers?

Ask customers this question—the answers may surprise you. Work through **Who You Help** diagnosis questions again or revisit Draft a Professional Identity (page 110). You may need additional feedback to clarify how the benefits you offer are connected to what past or present customers value.

Do the Benefits You Offer address the biggest, most important elements of the customer's job-to-be-done?

Do you understand the true job-to-be-done, or are you guessing at what it is? Can you reconceive/reposition or modify **What You Do** to focus on more sharply-defined **Benefits**?

Have you clearly defined the Benefits You Offer so you can communicate them? In what new ways could you create awareness or encourage evaluation (videos, social media, online presentations, etc.)? Are you enabling purchase and delivery in ways Customers prefer?

Could you deliver your Benefits through a different Channel?

Does your customer prefer the current **Channel**? Could you adapt **Benefits You Offer** for alternative delivery **Channels**? Could you change your **Benefits** from a service into a product, or vice-versa?

Do you enjoy delivering your Benefits to Customers?

If so, great! If not, revisit **Who You Are**, **What You Do**, or **Who You Help** and adjust to create greater satisfaction on your part.

What kind of relationships do Customers expect you to establish and maintain?

Are you communicating with **Customers** in ways they prefer—or in ways you prefer? Can you modify how are you interact or communicate to better match their preferences?

How do **Customers** find out about you?

How do **Customers** evaluate your services (or product)?

Do you enable **Customers** to buy in the way(s) they prefer?

How do you deliver your service or product?

How do you ensure post-purchase satisfaction?

How They Know You
Questions and Solution Starting Points

Can you offer different purchase options? Can you deliver through a new or different medium (online, podcast, video, in-person, product)? Could a partner build awareness or deliver on your behalf? Have you asked **Customers** how satisfied they are with your service or product?

If you are an employee, how are you creating awareness among potential new internal clients of the **Benefits You Offer**?

Through which channel(s) do you now create awareness and deliver **Benefits You Offer**?

Roles and Relationships
Questions and Solution Starting Points

What roles do you play with respect to different **Customers**? Include both desirable and undesirable roles.

Which is the primary goal of your **Roles and Relationships**: retention or acquisition?

If your primary goal is retention, does **What You Do** include gauging **Customer** satisfaction? (If satisfaction is low, see **Benefits You Offer** diagnosis questions.) If your goal is acquisition, do you need to add or grow selling or marketing-related actions to **What You Do**?

Can you clearly define the role you play with respect to each **Customer**? What steps have you taken to better understand how **Customers** perceive the role(s) you play?

Who Helps You
Questions and Solution Starting Points

Who helps you?
Who are your Key Partners?

Could a **Key Partner** take on a **Key Activity** or provide a **Key Resource** for you, or vice versa? Could you deepen the relationship or make it more strategic to lower **Costs** for you and/or your partner? Could you modify your **Benefits You Offer**—or create an altogether new **Benefits You Offer**—through a **Key Partner** alliance? Could a **Key Partner** serve as a channel partner for you?

If you lack a Key Partner, why?

Could you convert a colleague or someone else into a **Key Partner**? No one succeeds alone! If you are self-employed or run a business, could you obtain a critical resource/activity at a lower cost or with better efficiency/quality by acquiring it from a **Key Partner** rather than seeking it internally?

Costs and Consequences
Questions and Solution Starting Points

Which activities generate the highest soft Costs within your model?

Activities that generate excessively high soft costs suggest a mismatch between your Professional Identity, **Who You Are** and **What You Do**. Revisit these building blocks—or consider reworking your entire model.

What are the biggest Costs incurred under your current model?

Could you reduce costs by modifying **What You Do** or sharing it with a **Key Partner**? Could any activity be reduced or eliminated without adversely affecting **Benefits You Offer**? Could you significantly increase **Benefits You Offer** by investing more in a partner—or in **Who You Are**?

Compensation and Rewards
Questions and Solution Starting Points

Are you accepting low Compensation and Rewards because you undervalue the Benefits You Offer? Are you or the customer equating **What You Do** with **Benefits You Offer**, or misinterpreting the job-to-be-done? Work through **Customer** and **Benefits You Offer** diagnosis questions again to see if you can boost the value of **Benefits You Offer**.

Are your Compensation and Rewards too low? If so, work through the **Benefits You Offer** questions again to make sure the **Customer**'s interpretation of **Benefits You Offer** match your own. Then, consider negotiating a compensation increase or improved rewards (such as increased flexibility). If you decide to acquire or replace a **Customer**, you will need to add **Channel**-related activities. Also, review "maker mix" on page 116!

If your Costs could be reduced, would you consider your current Compensation and Rewards adequate? If so, can you reduce/modify **Activities** needed to serve the **Customer**? If not, consider finding a new or additional **Customer**, or revising your entire model.

Are Compensation and Rewards paid in the manner the Customer prefers? Or are Compensation and Rewards paid in the manner you prefer? Could you switch from an employee model to a contractor model? From a retainer model to a subscription model? Or vice-versa? Could you change your service into a product that could be sold, leased, licensed, or subscribed to? Could you receive payment in kind? Could you negotiate receiving **Benefits** that cost **Customers** little but are valuable to you?

Step 4. Modify Blocks and Evaluate Effects

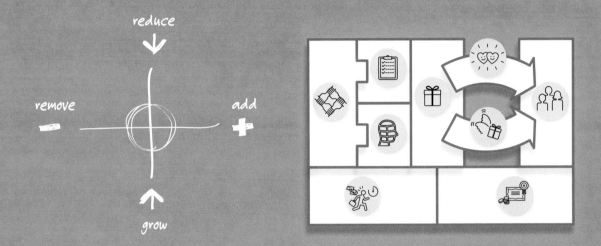

Refer to your responses to the Diagnosis Questions, then use the table on the right to list changes you'd like to make to your building blocks. For example, if you want to do less selling, in the What You Do row, write "Selling" under "Reduce."

For a complete overview of this technique, see the Four Actions Framework in *Blue Ocean Strategy* by Kim and Mauborgne.[16]

Building Block	Add +	Remove -	Grow ^	Reduce ˅
Who You Are				
What You Do				
Who You Help				
Benefits You Offer				
How They Know You and How You Deliver				
Roles and Relationships				
Who Helps You				
Compensation and Rewards				
Costs and Consequences				

Identifying the Effects of Building Block Changes

Identifying the effects of your changes is an intriguing—and sometimes complicated—process. That's because building blocks are interrelated: Changing an element in one building block requires changing an element in another block. We looked at this briefly in Chapter 2. Now, here's a more detailed primer on making changes and tracing their effects.

How Building Blocks Affect Each Other

Imagine a common problem with the Compensation and Rewards building block: not enough money coming in. You could bring in more money by 1) acquiring more/better/different Customers, 2) offering a more valuable Benefit, or 3) raising your fees. Let's assume you decide to increase Compensation by adding a new Customer. You would go back to the building block table on the previous page, and in the "Add" column next to "Who You Help," describe the new Customer you'd like to add.

So, let's say you've just added a Customer on paper. That's simple enough. But we can't count on new Customers to appear automatically, right? Adding a Customer usually requires additional outreach or marketing efforts. Therefore, you should make a corresponding entry to add or grow sales or marketing action next to What You Do.

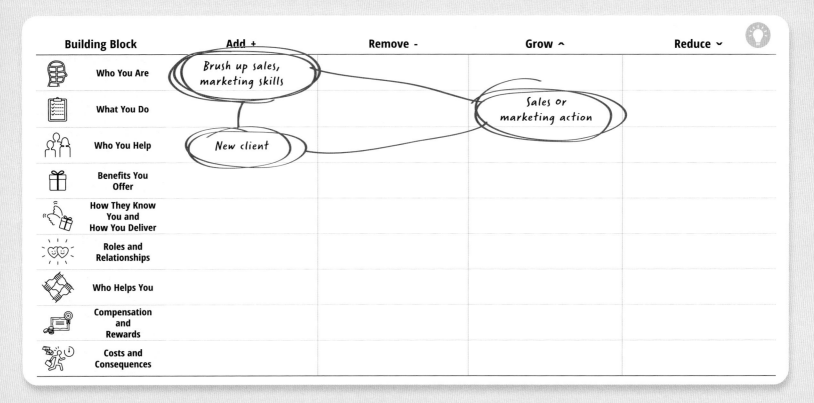

Building Block	Add +	Remove -	Grow ^	Reduce ⌄
Who You Are	Brush up sales, marketing skills			
What You Do			Sales or marketing action	
Who You Help	New client			
Benefits You Offer				
How They Know You and How You Deliver				
Roles and Relationships				
Who Helps You				
Compensation and Rewards				
Costs and Consequences				

This new entry under What You Do might itself affect other building blocks. For example, if you lack sales skills, you might want to undergo sales training or take a marketing course. You would then make an appropriate entry next to Who You Are as in the table on the opposite page.

On the other hand, you might accomplish your objective to boost sales by engaging a partner who is skilled in this area. You would then make an appropriate entry next to Who Helps You. Remember that you must pay Partners, too!

Here's the trick to effectively revising your work model: When you change an element in one building block to achieve a desired result, identify that change's impact on other building blocks. Then, modify elements in those other building blocks accordingly.

Here's a good way to accomplish this: in your mind's eye, imagine yourself taking the actions you've recorded here—make a mental "movie" of yourself acting upon your intentions. Then fast-forward that "movie" with respect to all related building blocks, in each block picturing what you see yourself doing differently. This will create more of an experiential sense of which changes are right for you.

Now, go through each block in your model that needs improving and make appropriate adjustments.

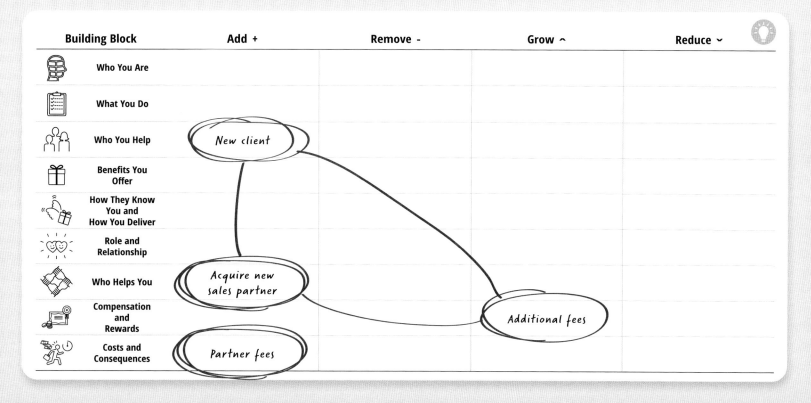

Building Block	Add +	Remove -	Grow ^	Reduce ⌄
Who You Are				
What You Do				
Who You Help	New client			
Benefits You Offer				
How They Know You and How You Deliver				
Role and Relationship				
Who Helps You	Acquire new sales partner			
Compensation and Rewards			Additional fees	
Costs and Consequences	Partner fees			

Step 5. Diagram Your "To-Be" Model

Once you've modified your hotspot building blocks, it's time to diagram a new work model. This is your to-be model—the next iteration along your career journey.

The more times you iterate a model, the stronger it becomes.

The Power of Prototyping

DO NOT diagram your work model once, then modify it once. The strength of the Work Model Canvas lies in providing a structured way to experiment with different models. It's a way to try out—to prototype—different work styles and discover what's best for you.

— Different Life Stages, Different Models —

Experimenting with multiple models helps when life changes.
What if your terrific manager is replaced tomorrow by the boss from hell?
Or, let's say you want to move into leadership
after spending years as a technical professional. Getting ready to retire?
Generating multiple options helps you quickly switch to a workable model
that gets you where you want to go.

Phil

Calculating Costs and Consequences

Phil was a Manchester-based freelance learning and development consultant who was hired via an employment agency to work full-time for the UK's national air traffic management service on a one-year contract. Phil's role was to train employees in new technology and processes that would help accomplish the service's mission to "keep the skies safe" while simultaneously reducing the instructional design burden on subject matter experts within the organisation.

"I loved it," says Phil. "Huge and interesting project, great colleagues, and pretty good pay. The only pain point was that their offices were located a five-hour drive away, so I had to take temporary accommodations there and drive home weekends."

At first, Phil worked mainly in person and on site. After COVID struck, he worked remotely from home using Microsoft's Teams videoconferencing platform.

Phil's contract was extended for a second full year, but the COVID epidemic had a massive impact on the service's income and many senior staff were let go in a restructuring. When the project started up again, Phil felt it had lost its bigger vision and been reduced to a bureaucratic exercise rife with seemingly endless video meetings, documentation, and box-ticking—but lacking the social contact and face-to-face relationships Phil had enjoyed when based in the service's offices. He was bored and felt that he was stagnating professionally.

"I know I was lucky to have paid work in a time of great uncertainty," Phil says, "but the job was making me miserable. Something had to change."

Then came a decisive blow: tax rule changes implemented by the UK government effectively slashed Phil's contractor income by 25%.

Phil sought help in a comprehensive series of work model training sessions, where his as-is work model showed pain points in stark relief:

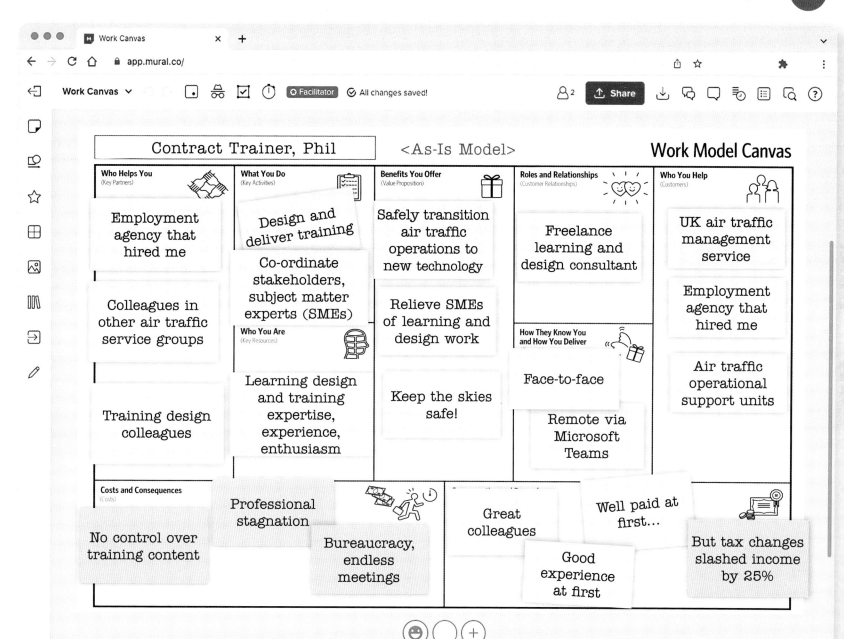

THE CONTRACT TRAINER

Phil started revising his work model.

He knew he could still earn the usual consultant day rates working either through agencies or directly with clients. But he wanted to move away from the money-for-time model and scale a new wholly-owned business where he could run workshops for his own clients using content of his choosing—including work modeling, entrepreneurial thinking, and innovation culture.

"This immediately highlighted marketing: an area where I'm weak—and do not enjoy at all—but which is vital for my revised model's success," says Phil. "So, I decided to get professional marketing help from Channel Partners so I can focus on the activities I'm good at and enjoy."

Phil completed his contract and is now working full-time on his new business.

"It's still early days, but things are progressing," he says. "Having a clear vision makes a tremendous difference."

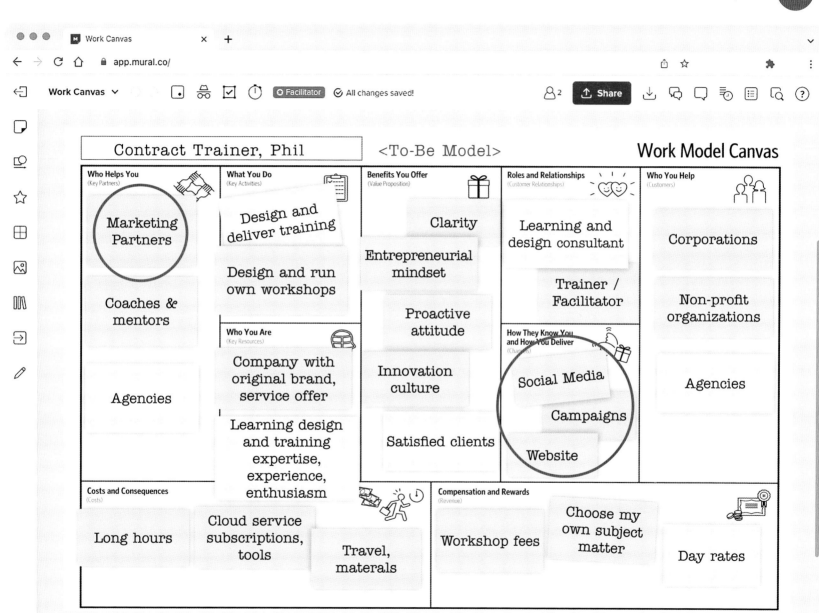

Work Model Canvas

Contract Trainer, Phil   <To-Be Model>

Who Helps You
(Key Partners)

- Marketing Partners
- Coaches & mentors
- Agencies

What You Do
(Key Activities)

- Design and deliver training
- Design and run own workshops

Who You Are
(Key Resources)

- Company with original brand, service offer
- Learning design and training expertise, experience, enthusiasm

Benefits You Offer
(Value Proposition)

- Clarity
- Entrepreneurial mindset
- Proactive attitude
- Innovation culture
- Satisfied clients

Roles and Relationships
(Customer Relationships)

- Learning and design consultant
- Trainer / Facilitator

How They Know You and How You Deliver
(Channels)

- Social Media
- Campaigns
- Website

Who You Help
(Customers)

- Corporations
- Non-profit organizations
- Agencies

Costs and Consequences
(Costs)

- Long hours
- Cloud service subscriptions, tools
- Travel, materials

Compensation and Rewards
(Revenue)

- Workshop fees
- Choose my own subject matter
- Day rates

Should You Become Self-Employed?

After working on your model, you may be wondering whether, like Phil, you should become wholly self-employed.

Almost everyone has dreamed of setting up their own business, launching a startup, or simply giving the boss notice and figuring out next steps later.

The upsides of becoming independently employed are clear: freedom, flexibility, and unbounded opportunity.

Downsides are possible, too: unstable earnings, isolation, and the potential to become trapped in an unending 24x7 workstyle.

In weighing the decision, thoughtful professionals often sense there is a hidden barrier to becoming self-employed—one they vaguely perceive but are unable to clearly describe. They believe that if they could identify this barrier and understand the challenges it presents, they could make a sensible go/no go decision.

Well, they are right. There is an unseen barrier—and it is real, identifiable, and addressable. The good news is that for most of us, three simple questions can quickly answer the "should I be self-employed?" question.

You can easily address these three questions because you understand the logic of how organizations deliver Benefits to Customers. In a nutshell, organizations create Benefits, then use Channels to communicate, sell, and deliver them to Customers:

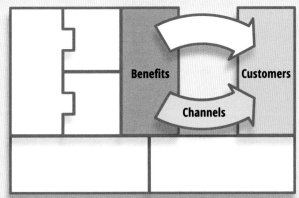

Here are critical points to keep in mind:

Organizations are successful only when they own or exert control over Channels that link Benefits to Customers

Note that Channels link organizations to Customers outside the organization (external Customers). Therefore, ownership or control over Channels is essential to the success of any enterprise, regardless of number of employees. Nothing happens without Channels. Lack of effective Channels is a showstopper for any organization.

Most professionals working inside organizations serve internal Customers: colleagues, partners, supervisors, and others

Relatively few deal directly with external Customers. In fact, organizational "jobs" are essentially Channels connecting individual professionals to internal (and sometimes external) Customers. Having a "job" as an employee of an organization eliminates the tough work of attracting and acquiring Customers and lets you concentrate on delivering Benefits. But when you give up a job and go solo, you can no longer focus only on delivery. You must now establish your own Channels to attract and acquire external Customers.

Do you see where this is going?

Here's the punchline: **The hidden barrier to going solo is Channels**. Whether you start a one-person business or launch a venture with others, you must take on the tough job of attracting and acquiring Customers.

Now that the hidden barrier is clear, here are the three questions to help you decide whether or not to take the leap yourself:

1. Do you own or control your own Channels now?

If so, you may be ready to step out on your own—especially if your Channel is a strong word-of-mouth personal and professional reputation. If not, move on to question two.

2. Can you develop your own Channels?

If so, start experimenting in preparation to go solo! If not, move on to question three.

3. Can you acquire strong Channels via partnership(s)?

If so, terrific! But reality-test your plans carefully with potential Channel partners and remember that **while 100% online Channels are useful for transacting and delivering, they still require you to attract and acquire Customers**. Underestimating the difficulty of attracting prospective clients and selling to them is one of the most common mistakes made by new entrepreneurs.

Here's the takeaway: if you do not yet own or control a good Channel and are unable or unwilling to either develop one or acquire one via a partnership, you will likely do better as an employee.

THE REAL ESTATE DEVELOPER

Rahul

Pivoting from Employee to Entrepreneur

When Bengaluru-based Rahul Sabharwal answered a call for advice from a friend living in the UK, he never imagined the conversation would end up triggering a revolution in his professional life.

Amid the global COVID lockdown, Rahul's London-based friend was conducting an increasingly frantic long-distance search for a safe community living arrangement for his retired parents in India. So, he turned to Rahul, who he knew was a expert in India's real estate market.

That expertise was hard won. Over a 25-year career, Rahul had achieved the position of Chief Operating Officer (COO) at VBHC, one of India's leading affordable condominium developers. Yet when his London friend called, Rahul was grappling with his own dilemma—and had sought help from a professional mentor.

That mentor was Vasanth Kumar, a former retailing executive who himself had made a career transition to coaching and mentoring budding entrepreneurs. At first, Rahul sought advice from Vasanth on how to achieve a CEO position within India's real estate industry. Vasanth recommended that together they diagram and examine the business model of Rahul's current employer and his role within that model.

Their visualization of VBHC's model revealed two big problems. First, diverse homebuyer backgrounds and the mix of resident and non-resident buyers resulted in post-sale conflicts between condominium management and owners or tenants. Yet as an employee, Rahul had limited influence over which customers VBHC—and the industry as a whole—chose to serve.

Vasanth

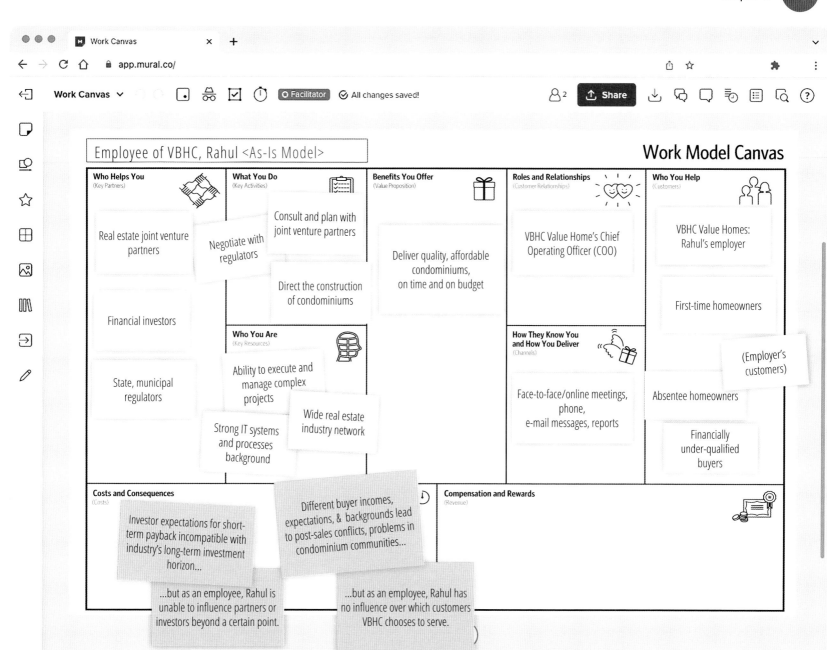

Employee of VBHC, Rahul <As-Is Model>

Work Model Canvas

Who Helps You (Key Partners)

- Real estate joint venture partners
- Financial investors
- State, municipal regulators

What You Do (Key Activities)

- Negotiate with regulators
- Consult and plan with joint venture partners
- Direct the construction of condominiums

Who You Are (Key Resources)

- Ability to execute and manage complex projects
- Strong IT systems and processes background
- Wide real estate industry network

Benefits You Offer (Value Proposition)

- Deliver quality, affordable condominiums, on time and on budget

Roles and Relationships (Customer Relationships)

- VBHC Value Home's Chief Operating Officer (COO)

How They Know You and How You Deliver (Channels)

- Face-to-face/online meetings, phone, e-mail messages, reports

Who You Help (Customers)

- VBHC Value Homes: Rahul's employer
- First-time homeowners
- (Employer's customers)
- Absentee homeowners
- Financially under-qualified buyers

Costs and Consequences (Costs)

- Investor expectations for short-term payback incompatible with industry's long-term investment horizon...
- Different buyer incomes, expectations, & backgrounds lead to post-sales conflicts, problems in condominium communities...
- ...but as an employee, Rahul is unable to influence partners or investors beyond a certain point.
- ...but as an employee, Rahul has no influence over which customers VBHC chooses to serve.

Compensation and Rewards (Revenue)

THE REAL ESTATE DEVELOPER

The second problem was that VBHC dealt with investors and partners whose expected timeframe for investment returns were incompatible with the industry's long-term investment horizon. Yet again, as an employee, Rahul had limited influence over VBHC's choice of partners and investors.

But Rahul's dilemma was even bigger. Together, the two thought partners realized that even if Rahul were to attain a CEO position, the structure of the residential condominium sector made it unlikely he could ever enjoy full autonomy in his choice of Customers, Channels, or Key Partners.

In the meantime, the worsening COVID epidemic had severely disrupted India's real estate market, causing Rahul to reflect on alternative real estate business models and contemplate his next career move more deeply.

During a meeting with Vasanth, Rahul wondered aloud whether he should explore starting a new venture of his own. Vasanth immediately corroborated the thought and pointed out that the only way to achieve true autonomy in choosing Customers and Key Partners was for Rahul to start his own company.

That statement snapped Rahul to attention: while investigating community living arrangements on behalf of his London-based friend, Rahul had been struck by how India's small but fast-growing retirement home development sector offered both Customer uniformity and investing congruence between developers and Key Partners.

What's more, Rahul had noticed, real estate developers that were building retirement communities typically lacked dedicated organizations to provide on-site dining, housekeeping, medical, and concierge services. Instead, they would piece together disparate groups of local subcontractors to serve each new community. That often resulted in uneven or even substandard service. Could this be an opportunity to start a venture of his own?

Mentor and mentee set to work on a to-be model to refine and ultimately capture Rahul's thinking. The new model exploited Rahul's existing real estate sector knowledge and network to offer a powerful new Value Proposition: an outstanding end-to-end Customer experience for retirement home developers.

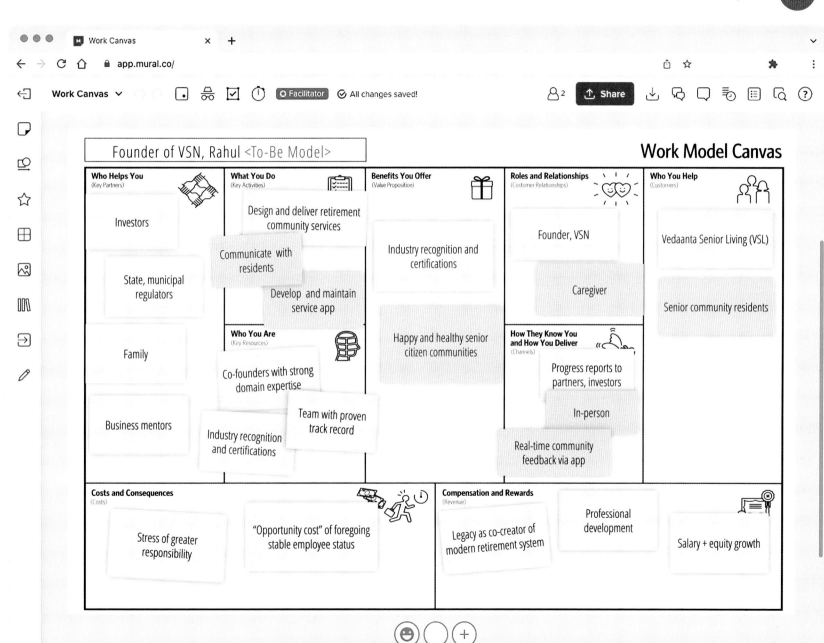

Work Model Canvas

Founder of VSN, Rahul <To-Be Model>

Who Helps You (Key Partners)
- Investors
- State, municipal regulators
- Family
- Business mentors

What You Do (Key Activities)
- Design and deliver retirement community services
- Communicate with residents
- Develop and maintain service app

Who You Are (Key Resources)
- Co-founders with strong domain expertise
- Team with proven track record
- Industry recognition and certifications

Benefits You Offer (Value Proposition)
- Industry recognition and certifications
- Happy and healthy senior citizen communities

Roles and Relationships (Customer Relationships)
- Founder, VSN
- Caregiver

How They Know You and How You Deliver (Channels)
- Progress reports to partners, investors
- In-person
- Real-time community feedback via app

Who You Help (Customers)
- Vedaanta Senior Living (VSL)
- Senior community residents

Costs and Consequences (Costs)
- Stress of greater responsibility
- "Opportunity cost" of foregoing stable employee status

Compensation and Rewards (Revenue)
- Legacy as co-creator of modern retirement system
- Professional development
- Salary + equity growth

Today Rahul serves as founder and CEO of Vedaanta Senior Needz (VSN), the dedicated customer and project acquisition division of Vedaanta Senior Living, one of India's fastest-growing retirement community service providers.

Vasanth continues to mentor Rahul in his quest to create a much-improved retirement living ecosystem in India.

Pause and ask yourself:

1 Have I done a quick revision without tracing how to-be changes ripple throughout the model? Have I truly grasped the implications of the changes by making a mental movie of myself enacting each building block revision?

2 Would I benefit from a thought partner viewing my model and asking questions?

3 Am I prepared to test Customer, Benefit, or Channel revisions with actual or prospective Customers?

4 Am I afraid to substantially rework or design more than one model? Am I aware that I'm learning **how to model**, not simply trying to create one "correct" model?

5 Can I access and influence the Channels I describe? Just because I can describe them doesn't mean I enjoy access to and influence over them.

The next chapter focuses on ways to test your revised model to see if it matches market reality. You may discover, as Eric did, that testing his revised model was simple: he simply created a proposal and presented it to his boss (though Eric's story doesn't end there!).

But if you seek a bigger change in your work, you will need to move beyond desktop tools—and use Outward Focus. Chapter 6 shows you how.

CHAPTER 6

Now, Test Your Work Model

Eric Tests
His Revised
Model

An Unexpected Response

Eric sat down opposite Jan, his supervisor. The whirlwind pace of EPIC's operations left little room for small talk, so Eric was unsurprised when Jan got immediately to the point. But what she said caught him completely off guard.

"I've read your proposal, Eric, and it makes perfect sense," she said, shuffling a thin sheaf of PowerPoint printouts on her desk. "How would you like to proceed?"

Erik found himself momentarily speechless. He had been expecting to go over his proposal page by page and respond to questions. "Well…, uh…that's great!" he stammered.

Jan flashed a knowing smile. "You didn't expect such quick approval."

Eric nodded.

"The benefit to EPIC you propose is important and timely," she continued. "We need a pipeline of up-and-coming senior systems engineers. And we need people like you who both recognize that need and can act on it."

"Let me suggest next steps," she went on. "First, you need to train a successor who can take over your current role. I recommend you hold trainings for some of our junior systems engineers, then accompany the most promising ones to oversee their first on-site installs. After that, you can phase out your travel responsibilities while ramping up formal training sessions. How does that sound?"

Jan was moving so quickly Eric was at a loss for words. He nodded again.

"Good," said Jan. "I've got four system engineers in mind for your first training session. How about we start December 4?"

Only three weeks from today, Eric thought. He felt a mild wave of panic starting to creep over him. He fought it off, exerting himself to sound confident. "Uh, sure—I can do that," he replied.

"Excellent!" said Jan. "I'll mail you the details. This is a big step for you, Eric. Your proposal showed real initiative."

"Thank you for the opportunity, Jan," Eric replied.

Eric stepped out of Jan's office, hardly believing his good luck. *Maybe it's like the coach said,* he thought to himself. *When you take action, things happen.* He strode down the hallway whistling his favorite Weezer tune.

Eric Iterates

December 4 found Eric in a presentation room, nervously testing laptop, projector, and remote clicker, and rearranging oversized printed charts in preparation for his first training session. He had arrived two hours early.

At the appointed time, Eric began presenting to four young systems engineers. He showed a long series of text-heavy PowerPoint slides, explained system requirements and pre-install procedures in detail, and covered EPIC's security and privacy policies, speaking nonstop for almost 90 minutes before pausing for Q&A. He was surprised to answer only two perfunctory questions about the next training date and homework before dismissing the class.

The next day Jan called Eric into her office. "How did it go?" she asked.

"Well, OK, I guess," said Eric. "I was a little nervous."

"I've had some participant feedback," said Jan, handing Eric her cell phone. "Read this."

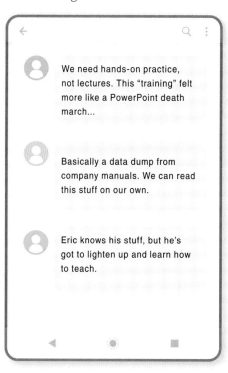

We need hands-on practice, not lectures. This "training" felt more like a PowerPoint death march...

Basically a data dump from company manuals. We can read this stuff on our own.

Eric knows his stuff, but he's got to lighten up and learn how to teach.

Eric flushed red and felt his ears burn.

"Don't worry!" laughed Jan. "You should have seen the first training I ever did. It was horrendous!"

"To tell the truth, I've never done formal training," Eric admitted. "That part of my work model was untested."

"Nonsense!" said Jan. "You've done nearly one hundred installs, and every time there was a hospital IT manager there to observe and learn, right?"

Eric nodded in agreement.

"Well, why not run the sessions like a collaborative install? You could play the role of hospital IT manager. Have the SEs explain to you what they are doing as they install on test servers right in class. You can oversee the activity, do a debriefing, then give them some sample challenges, like *What questions would you ask a hospital IT manager in order to troubleshoot this particular installation problem?* You've got to develop their thinking styles, not just their instruction-following behavior."

Eric's face brightened. "That makes sense, Jan. I'll rework my approach—let's touch base again after the next session and see how it's going."

Immediately following Eric's next training session, Jan sent him a two-character text message, which read: "??"

Eric replied: "!!"

What If Your Situation Differs from Eric's?

Maybe your organization or boss is less supportive than Eric's, and you worry that proposing a role change for yourself might be rejected. But consider that almost all employers make an important calculation when considering changes designed to accommodate a valued employee: *replacement costs.*

Do you know what it would cost your employer to replace you if you quit? The Society for Human Resource Management (SHRM) reports that on average the cost to an organization to replace an employee is six to nine months of that employee's salary. For an employee who earns $60,000 per year, that means the employer must spend between $30,000 and $45,000 to recruit and train a replacement. And that assumes a suitable replacement is available in the current labor market! These costs can rise significantly for specialized professionals because replacement candidates often demand high compensation when approached by recruiters.

Employers also risk losing valuable experience—and difficult-to-replace institutional knowledge—when replacing employees. What's more, productivity usually suffers while replacement employees are being trained or onboarded.

So, if your as-is work model shows that you are 1) capable, and 2) delivering value to the enterprise—and you are proposing a new way to do just that—replacing you is the last thing your employer wants to do. Just be sure your proposal covers potential successors or partners who could take over your role, including a plan to help with training or onboarding those people.

A Simple Test? Or Something More Rigorous?

If, like Eric, you're a competent professional making relatively minor modifications to your work model, you may be ready to test it now.

Like Eric, you'll want to discuss your to-be model with a thought partner, and like Eric, you may want to write a formal proposal or craft a presentation for a supervisor, colleague, or partner. But the test itself may be as simple as sending the proposal or delivering the presentation to the appropriate person. And, like Eric, you may discover that you need to "test" your new role!

Keep in mind that not every potential course of action needs formal "testing." For example, if you want to write an e-mail message to your sister, the best "test" is simply to write the message itself—then hit "send."

Even when it comes to career-related action, the test of your revised model could be as simple as asking your supervisor for permission to dedicate two hours of your time each week to a new project of interest, seeking approval to shadow someone in a different department, or requesting authorization to work from home (or in the office) an extra day per week. Approval of any of these actions could lead to solid progress in your professional life.

On the other hand, your revised to-be model may call for a significant change. You may want to move into an entirely different area of your organization, or away from a supervisory or team relationship that no longer works well. You may be thinking about leaving your organization altogether or starting your own enterprise. You may be considering changing industries or even occupations. Maybe you're contemplating retirement in some form: with a reduced workload or a brand-new workstyle.

Such changes call for more rigorous testing of your to-be model because the stakes are higher: you want to make sure your model matches market reality before assuming the risk of acting on it. The riskiest way to test a to-be model is by accepting a job offer before truly understanding either your own model or the new employer's enterprise model. You might end up relocating your same "hotspots" to a new desk—or discovering that the new organization is a poor fit.

Avoid this by recognizing that on paper a to-be work model usually contains a number of *unvalidated hypotheses* within its building blocks: it is an untested proposal to help others while doing good things for yourself.

The most practical way to test new work models is to 1) find and contact people who represent or are knowledgeable about the client(s) you want to serve, then 2) talk with them in a structured way about the workplace, industry, or professional problems they face. Let's look at a powerful way to do just that.

The Valuable Work Detector

As an employee Eric naturally enjoyed insider knowledge of EPIC and the problems, issues, needs, and industry trends it faced. But you may be considering moving to a new job, a new organization or industry—or even starting your own venture. If so, you need to grasp some of the problems, issues, needs, and industry trends faced by those who will be served by your work model.

We like to say that *valuable work lurks behind Problems, Issues, Needs, and Trends*—or **PINT** for short. Here are definitions of the four **PINT** elements:

1. Problems or Potential

Something is broken or not working well, or an opportunity exists for something new. For example, organizations in a certain industry are experiencing the problem of excessive employee turnover.

2. Issues

Nothing is broken, but rules, regulations, or other external conditions are changing. For example, upcoming legislation seems certain to change how an enterprise can employ foreign graduate students as interns or contract workers.

3. Needs

Something is missing, or there is a desire for something new or different. For example, an employer planning to enter South American markets needs talented, culturally sensitive employees with Spanish and Portuguese language skills.

4. Trends

Things are changing or moving in new directions, or people are behaving differently. For example, the growing use of miniature cameras and other devices in healthcare suggests that a medical equipment manufacturer needs more engineers with robotics expertise.

Accurately identifying the Problems, Issues, Needs, or Trends faced by prospective Customers is the essence of valuable work detection. If you can do this in just one or two **PINT** categories, you're close to locating valuable work.

The next step is to clearly describe how your model responds to the Problems, Issues, Needs, or Trends you've identified. For example, if you have identified a Problem, your model might provide a solution. If you have identified an Issue, your model might provide an innovation. If you have identified a Need, your model might furnish a resource. And if you have accurately spotted a Trend, your model might provide a powerful positioning idea.

These four responses—**S**olutions, **I**nnovations, **R**esources, and **P**ositioning ideas—go by the acronym **SIRP**. Here are definitions of the four **SIRP** elements:

1. Solutions or Suggestions

A fix, repair, or recommendation for a new method, service, or product that addresses a **Problem or Potential**. For example, you might recommend that an organization implement flexible scheduling after exit interviews showed key employees had left to seek more accommodating work hours.

2. Innovations

Proactively adapting procedures to address an **Issue**. For example, you might propose expanding recruitment targets to promising new domestic graduate engineering programs, thus reducing dependence on engineers trained overseas.

3. Resources

People, money, materials, or intellectual property that satisfies a **Need**. You yourself may have the cultural sensitivity and language skills needed for the employer seeking to enter South American markets.

4. Positioning Ideas

A proposed way to exploit a **Trend** *or minimize risk.* For example, you might propose that the manufacturer endow a robotics engineering professorship at a key graduate school to ensure a talent pipeline.

The **Valuable Work Detector** is a simple tool for organizing a search for Problems, Issues, Needs, and Trends that you can address with Solutions, Innovations, Resources, or Positioning Ideas.

You can use the Valuable Work Detector without putting content into every box. Just record **PINT** or **SIRP** elements you discover while talking with experts or prospective clients.

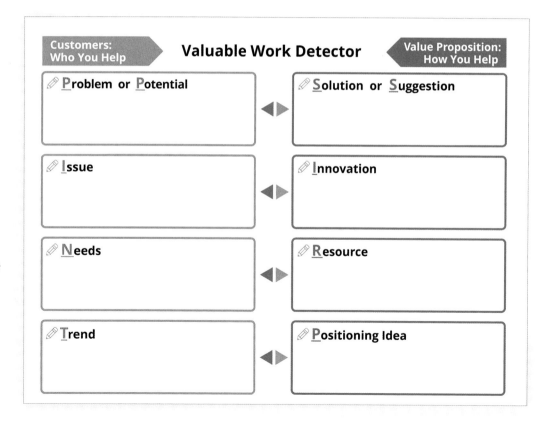

THE TRANSPORTATION ENGINEER

Testing Detects More Valuable Work

Wayne was a 39-year-old senior transportation engineer at DKS Engineering who became discouraged about his career when his team lost two key bids to competitors. He contacted Jim, vice president of human resources at DKS, and asked for a confidential consultation.

Jim and Wayne discussed Wayne's reputation within DKS as that of "firm nerd." Though not an information technology professional per se, Wayne had suggested many of the tools that improved DKS Engineering's use of cloud technology. Jim asked Wayne to complete a to-be work model and a professional identity exercise and return two days later for another conference. At their second meeting, Wayne presented Jim with the following Professional Identity description:

> I notice trends buried in tons of data we collect: I'm a data tamer who makes the technically mysterious seem friendly. I turn data into information that clients use to make decisions and solve real transportation problems. I create applied results that make clients smile and shake their heads with amazement.

Wayne

For his Professional Identity tag line, Wayne had written:

> Nerd who creates insights by telling stories with data.

Jim and Wayne discussed how Wayne's statements fit into his revised work model, then turned their attention to topics identified at a recent DKS strategic planning retreat.

DKS had foreseen that computer-driven cars would come to cities sooner than expected, and that smart highways and ubiquitous embedded monitors would eventually tell the moment-to-moment story of where people were and where they wanted to go. But preparing for all this would require tremendous amounts of engineering and data science work—work DKS was well-positioned to undertake.

At the retreat, therefore, DKS had modified its enterprise business model by formally adding a new Key Resource (big data analysis capability), a new Key Activity (design smart transportation systems for cities), and a new Value Proposition (provide cities with cloud-based smart transportation grids that can double the people-moving capacity of existing infrastructure).

Jim asked Wayne to post an oversized Valuable Work Detector on the office wall and write in at least one element related to DKS's latest strategy decision. Wayne quickly matched his work model's Benefits Offered and Who You Are elements with three of the four PINT elements:

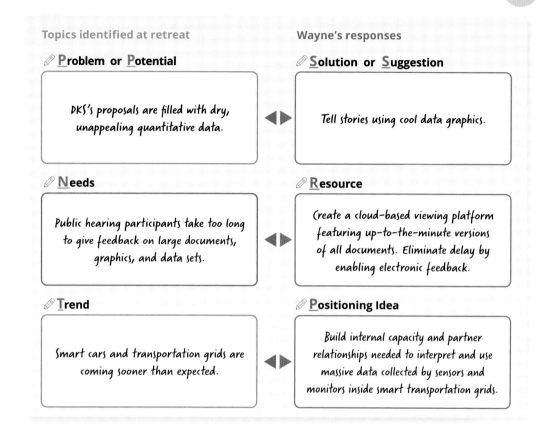

Topics identified at retreat

✎ **P**roblem or **P**otential

DKS's proposals are filled with dry, unappealing quantitative data.

✎ **N**eeds

Public hearing participants take too long to give feedback on large documents, graphics, and data sets.

✎ **T**rend

Smart cars and transportation grids are coming sooner than expected.

Wayne's responses

✎ **S**olution or **S**uggestion

Tell stories using cool data graphics.

✎ **R**esource

Create a cloud-based viewing platform featuring up-to-the-minute versions of all documents. Eliminate delay by enabling electronic feedback.

✎ **P**ositioning Idea

Build internal capacity and partner relationships needed to interpret and use massive data collected by sensors and monitors inside smart transportation grids.

Within the hour both men saw, with startling clarity, that Wayne was ideally positioned to head up the new smart transportation systems initiative within DKS. Wayne was able to validate his to-be work model and strengthen his Benefits Offered by adding "Build DKS's new service capacity."

Days later Wayne's transfer within DKS initiative was official.

Let's move to testing your model in the broader marketplace of valuable work: work that lies outside your current workplace or existing clientele. As you proceed, use the Valuable Work Detector to describe the purpose of your work and how it addresses Problems, Issues, Needs, and Trends on behalf of Customers. In the process you'll gain additional insights about target clients that you can add to your Valuable Work Detector.

How to Test Models

Testing means identifying assumptions in a model, then getting feedback from people who are in a position to distinguish assumptions from facts. Feedback needs to come from domain experts or potential customers, not from friends or family. Here's an overview of the process:

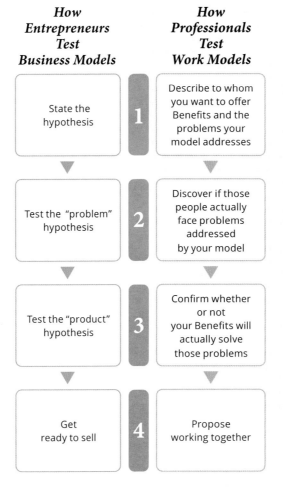

How Entrepreneurs Test Business Models		*How Professionals Test Work Models*
State the hypothesis	**1**	Describe to whom you want to offer Benefits and the problems your model addresses
Test the "problem" hypothesis	**2**	Discover if those people actually face problems addressed by your model
Test the "product" hypothesis	**3**	Confirm whether or not your Benefits will actually solve those problems
Get ready to sell	**4**	Propose working together

The Why of Testing

Serial entrepreneur and startup guru Steve Blank developed a robust, repeatable process for figuring out what **Customers** need and are willing to buy. Blank's process is important because many companies (and unsuccessful entrepreneurs) focus on developing and selling services or products before truly understanding potential **Customers**.[17]

For instance, when Motorola failed to discover whether prospective **Customers** wanted a global, satellite-based mobile telephone system, it lost U.S. $5 billion (yes, billion) developing and launching its Iridium service. Similarly, R.J. Reynolds lost U.S. $450 million on its Premier and Eclipse smokeless cigarettes: Nonsmokers loved the idea—but **Customers** (smokers!) couldn't have cared less.[18]

Remember: like Motorola and R.J. Reynolds, companies and entrepreneurs have assumptions about problems and solutions. But **Customers** have facts. And facts often show that we need to modify our assumptions.

That's why smart entrepreneurs thoroughly test and validate their models before executing. We will all do well to follow their example and test our work models.

Following the diagram on the opposite page, here's how you might test the business model for a new software application. **First, state the hypothesis**: "Hiring managers are overwhelmed by having to submit listings to multiple job services, then track all the responses. They need an app that simultaneously submits listings to multiple services then automatically tracks responses, showing everything on one convenient dashboard."

Second, test the "problem" hypothesis by talking with potential users or experts to see if hiring managers actually face such a problem (they may not—or they may already use a solution you didn't know about).

Third, test the "product" hypothesis by speaking with experts to discover whether or not your app—the "product"—would actually solve the problem (it might not).

Finally, get ready to sell by making adjustments to the app to overcome objections or add needed functionality.

Testing a work model uses the same logic but is less complicated. To test a work model, you (1) describe to whom you want to offer **Benefits**, (2) talk with clients or experts to see if potential **Customers** actually face the problems addressed by your model, (3) confirm whether or not your **Benefits Offered**

will actually solve those problems, and (4) propose working together.

The key to testing is *acting on feedback received.* During Step 2 on the facing page, for example, you might learn through that potential clients do NOT experience the problems addressed by your model. If so, you must go back and modify either Benefits Offered or Customers.

Even if potential clients do experience the problems your model addresses, in Step 3 you might discover that your Benefits Offered do not address them adequately or in the way they prefer. Again, you must go back and modify the model to match market reality.

Keep in mind that one interviewee's opinion represents only a single data point. But similar opinions from multiple experts or potential clients is a strong indication of *the market view—not your personal view or one particular professional's view*. That's why it's important to speak with several people rather than just one or two.

When your model seems to match market reality, you can try "selling" to a **Customer** (more on this soon). If they don't buy, pivot (start over) and modify your model to overcome reasons given for not buying. Repeat. When a **Customer** "buys," you are

hired—or ready to take on other new **Customers**.

What should you do if your revised work model is a mismatch with market reality, but revising it enough to make it match would mean creating a model you don't like or find uninteresting?

Well, maybe you need to test your model more thoroughly, or in a different industry—or with people in different functional roles. Maybe your personal "brand" is not resonating—run the Brand Fitness Test described on page 195. Or you may need to develop new skills or a better track record of accomplishment in your field, or in a different field. The harsh truth is that markets rarely pay us to do exactly whatever it is we want to do, and that EVERY form of work—no matter how exciting, interesting, or prestigious—requires performing *some* unenjoyable tasks.

With that caveat, let's see how one woman tested a brand new to-be model.

Cyd Tests Her Model

Two words on Cyd Cannizzaro's offbeat calling card drew laughs—and curiosity about her work goals.

For years, Cyd had enjoyed frequent chats about garbage and recycling with a friend who shared her passion for environmental issues, and the two laughingly dubbed their discussions "talkin' trash."

But when Cyd was laid off from her job as a customer service trainer, she decided trash talk should be more than a pastime; it should be her vocation. Cyd vowed to find work focused on environmental issues: "work that makes a difference," she called it.

Cyd started testing a new work model by reaffirming her goal: helping others recycle and dispose of waste responsibly. The next step was to meet people and share that goal.

Because she was unaffiliated with a recycling organization, Cyd created a memorable, two-word calling card that defined her goal and expressed her personality. "Talkin' Trash" resonated as an introduction at public meetings about solid waste disposal, green product conventions, community recycling, and other events.

Cyd doggedly pursued her goal, at first taking a job at a natural foods market where she could put some of her recycling ideas into practice. In the meantime, she kept tweaking her model in response to feedback from industry professionals.

Then one day her message resonated with members of a municipal task force on sustainability. That led to a full-time recycling coordinator position for a city near her home. Ever since—and through a series of increasingly responsible roles at different organizations—Cyd Cannizzaro has been "talkin' trash" for a living.

Cyd

Steve Blank calls it "getting out of the building." Career professionals call it "networking." They mean the same thing: contacting and meeting with experts, potential clients, or people who can introduce you to experts or potential clients for the purpose of discovering whether or not your model is viable.

The key to effective testing is to avoid "selling." Your meetings should focus on validating your work model assumptions *from the Customer's perspective.* As Steve Blank says, don't try to convince Customers that they have the problems or opportunities you think they do!

Who to Approach and What to Say

> **Hip Tip:**
> Keep careful track of who referred you to whom— and be sure to thank them!

Most professionals are interested in talking with other professionals about topics of mutual interest. We suggest calling on the telephone. As a rule of thumb, many professionals, especially older people, welcome voice communications over electronic inquiries: voice calls are warmer, less expected, and indicate greater effort and care on the part of the caller. But use your judgment. E-mail or other digital communications may be preferred by professionals of any age depending on industry or personal workstyle.

Start with friendly first contacts: Talk with family, friends, colleagues, neighbors, church or professional association members, and others in your personal network. Tell them you're reshaping your career around new service goals.

Ask them if they know anyone who might have a professional interest in these goals. Get as many names and contact particulars as you can. These newly obtained names are your *referrals.*

Next, contact your new referrals. The basic principle is to approach people through "warm" contacts—friends or colleagues of friends—or at least acquaintances of acquaintances. Avoid "cold calling"—approaching people without an introduction.

> *Everything great that happens in your career always starts with someone you know. You don't need to surf the Internet. Your next big break will not come from some mysterious technology, or discovery of new information. Your next big break will come from someone you know. Go know people.*
>
> — Derek Sivers

Script for a First-Time Referral Contact

Take a deep breath, pick up the phone (or prepare to hit "send"), using language along these lines:

Hello, Maryellen, this is Elsa Portillo. I was referred to you by Sally McCormick. I'm a logistics professional keen on new ways of implementing sustainability practices organization-wide. I understand you're an expert in this area, and I'm intrigued to know more about how you and your company address this issue. Would you have 20 minutes to get together for coffee or on Zoom sometime next week, maybe Tuesday or Wednesday in the late afternoon?

Exhale. Relax. Wait for the reply. If you've spoken sincerely, you'll get a positive response.

If the other party sounds hesitant or asks for details, tell them how they can benefit from meeting with you:

I thought you could offer some insight into this issue, and in exchange I'd be happy to share some original ideas and my perspective on the future of sustainable logistics. Would late afternoon next Tuesday or Wednesday suit you?

If she agrees, schedule the meeting. If not, ask her for a referral, thank her for her time and move on.

That's all there is to it. Many people find this kind of calling difficult—even agonizing. *But if you make six calls like this, things will happen.*

Meet Your Referrals

What do you say when meeting with a new referral for the first time? One reliable icebreaker is to acknowledge your mutual acquaintance ("So, Maryellen, I understand you went to school with Sally...") But keep the pleasantries short. Remember, you asked for 20 minutes, so stick to the schedule.

Here are some prompts to jumpstart the discussion and help you start understanding your interviewee's personal or organizational business model:

"**Tell me how you got started** in logistics and what brought you to Prospect Corporation." "**How are you pursuing** your sustainability goals today?"

"**Who shares your problems and concerns** with respect to sustainability? Customers? Suppliers? Regulators? Community members?" "**How do you measure economic impact?**"

If you're lucky, the interviewee may hint or even talk openly about a job-to-be-done, a Key Partner, or another aspect of their organization. If so, **ask clarifying questions** and restate the interviewee's thoughts until they agree with your interpretation. Clarify the interviewee's thoughts now, because afterwards you'll want to concentrate on researching and preparing a proposal to work with this person, not rethinking what was said.

The interviewee may even ask about your **Benefits Offered** or another aspect of your model.

If the interview is going **extremely** well—and depending upon the formality of the situation and the scope of help you might offer—you may want to suggest working together right then and there. If so, be ready to discuss specifics of how you can help.

If you sense a written proposal would be appropriate, tell the interviewee that you have ideas about how to help and you'd like their approval to submit a proposal. Deep interest in your prospect's goals—and positioning yourself as someone who can become part of the solution—will bring you and your prospective Customer closer together.

The Secret Question

Here's a secret question with seemingly miraculous power to elicit deep insights from ordinary conversations. The key is to ask this question at the end of an interview, not in the middle:

"What else should I know about ... ?"

For example, near the end of her interview (page 168), Elsa should be sure to ask Maryellen:

"So, what else should I know about implementing sustainable practices in a company like Prospect?"

Why is this question so powerful? Most professionals harbor pet theories about the challenges, opportunities, and ups and downs of their professions, and they welcome opportunities to share those thoughts. You simply provide the invitation—as a sincere listener eager to hear insights gleaned from your interviewee's hard-earned experience.

Before the interview is over, be sure to:

1. Explain, then solicit feedback on the **Benefits you offer**
2. Ask for at least one new referral who might be interested in those **Benefits**—and for permission to use the interviewee's name when contacting that referral

After each meeting, **compare the assumptions in your model with new facts you've acquired**. Reflect on what you learned and record insights in your Valuable Work Detector or elsewhere. After several such meetings, you should have a good idea which assumptions need adjusting. And of course, send a thank you note to your interviewee.

What to Do if Your Work Model Fails to Resonate

When you share your model, do listeners perk up and sit straighter in their chairs? If not, several factors may be at work.

Is your model emotionally compelling? If not, make sure the language you're using is simple, understandable, and appropriate for the professional environment(s) you are targeting. Sometimes good copywriting makes a dramatic difference.

Does your model address real economic problems or opportunities? Few organizations spend money purely for social or political reasons. Clarify or rethink how your model makes an economic difference to **Customers**.

Are you a credible proponent of your model? Can **Customers** be confident you have the drive, track record, expertise, and skills—the Key Resources—needed to implement your model? If you're unsure how potential **Customers** perceive you, ask! (see page 109). And make sure to work through the next chapter on personal branding.

The Financial "Plumber"

After being laid off, Jan Kimmel, a seasoned businesswoman with a physics degree, decided her new model would blend finance with operations. "The two disciplines rarely go together," says Jan, "but they should." Unfortunately, her newly defined goal failed to resonate with informational interviewees. So, Jan developed a memorable elevator pitch:

*I'm a **financial plumber**. I locate leaks and clogs in a company's financial system and partner with operations to make needed repairs and keep profits flowing.*

Jan's metaphors may sound corny, but they resonated with fresh manufacturing sector contacts. Jan accepted a full-time position with a high-precision manufacturer, blending—you guessed it—finance and operations.

You've found and met with people from interesting organizations, some of whom would probably make good **Customers**. If you feel ready to sell, and are enthusiastic about acquiring a specific organization as a **Customer**, here are recommended next steps:

1. Research the organization, diagram its enterprise model, and visually show how you fit into and can contribute to that model

2. Arrange an interview with a decision-maker

3. Propose to help the organization with a specific project or initiative

Ways to investigate prospective **Customers** include attending trade shows or industry events, talking with experts or analysts, visiting organizations in "adjacent" industry sectors, and reading professional or popular publications in the prospect's field. Your goal is to put **yourself** in the prospect's place and learn to see the rest of the world—and yourself—through their eyes. And remember, ask the secret question each time you talk with a new contact!

How to Obtain "Insider" Data

Let's focus on one of your secret weapons: your ability to recognize, describe, and analyze business models. What better way to understand a prospective Customer than to draw its business model?

If your prospective **Customer** is listed on a U.S. stock market and required to file documents with the United States Securities and Exchange Commission (SEC), query the EDGAR database (search "EDGAR and SEC"), a free public resource generally known only to investors, MBAs, and savvy businesspeople. You'll discover an astonishing array of financial and strategic information about your prospect.

Diagram the business models of one or two of the prospective **Customers** you've identified—and experiment by adding, removing, growing, or reducing different building block elements.

Try to concisely define their Value Proposition and figure out which building blocks might contain "pain points." Imagine competitive pressures they may be facing. Could they respond effectively by altering elements of their business model? (Incidentally, their competitors may be good prospective **Customers**, too.)

One surefire "pain point" is financial: Most organizations are eager to increase Revenue or reduce Costs. Try to quantify—at least roughly—the positive economic effect your Benefits could have on the organization if it were to hire you.

You might start by defining an important **job** you believe your prospective **Customer** needs to get done. Then work backwards: What **Benefits** would help the **Customer** with that job? What **Key Activities** could you perform to contribute to their **Value Proposition**? Do you have the necessary Resources? If not, could you enlist the help of a Key Partner? Can you show how external forces are affecting the Customer's business model, and if so, could you help them adjust? Now's the time to unleash the power of business model thinking on behalf of prospective **Customers**—and yourself.

Your goal is to meet with and sell your work model to a decision-maker in the prospective **Customer**'s organization. Use networking techniques to secure an appointment, but in this interview, focus sharply on a specific aspect of your model that can help your prospect. Your goal is to propose working for the **Customer**. If the interviewee rejects your proposal, you can "pivot" and revisit your model.

Approach your decision-maker through the warmest possible referrals. If your networking efforts haven't yet yielded someone who works directly with your potential **Customer**, by now you should be familiar enough with your target sector to make a connection with a bit more networking.

On the other hand, directly and boldly approaching a decision-maker without any introduction whatsoever may be the most powerful choice, depending on the industry and/or personalities involved.

When contacting decision-makers you might say something like, "I think you have a significant opportunity to [...] and I have some specific ideas you may find powerful. Can we get together?"

If you've followed business model testing principles up to this point, you're likely to enjoy a warm reception.

Behavior That Wins Appointments

However you decide to go about approaching decision-makers, these findings from a study by the National Sales Executive Association might change your behavior:

- 2% of sales are made on the first contact
- 3% on the second contact
- 5% on the third contact
- 10% on the fourth contact
- 80% of sales are made on the fifth through 12th contact

Avoid the temptation to give up just because your second, third, or fourth attempt goes unanswered. Persistence produces appointments.

When you meet the decision-maker, state your understanding of the job-to-be-done in general terms, then prompt the interviewee for validation or correction. If your understanding is correct, the interviewee might say something like, "How would you recommend we solve this problem?" Just what you want to hear!

On the other hand, if your understanding wasn't entirely accurate, your interviewee may elaborate on the real opportunities or problems their organization faces. Regardless of how the interview unfolds, stick to your goal of proposing to help.

Depending on circumstances and the formality of the situation, you could make a verbal or written proposal to help.

If the interviewee accepts your offer to submit a written proposal, promise to deliver the document in a week or less. Then thank the interviewee and exit gracefully. Be sure to follow up with a brief "thank you" e-mail confirming 1) the agreed-upon nature of your proposal, and 2) when you will deliver it.

If the interviewee declines your offer to help, it's time to approach a different prospective Customer. If multiple prospects decline your offer, it may be time to "pivot" and revise your work model to better meet Customer needs.

The One-Page Proposal

Decision-makers love brevity and concision, so make your proposal compelling by summarizing it on a single page. Note: Your concise, single-page overview must signal a reserve of detail you can later present either in person or in a longer document.

Pivoting is the appropriate response to failing to sell to a prospective **Customer**. It means improving your work model's viability by modifying one or more building block elements. For example, you may decide to find an entirely new Customer, as Cyd did (page 166). Or, like Phil, you may decide to modify your Channels (page 142). Then again, you may need to rethink multiple building blocks, the way Dennis did in the case on the next page.

Pivoting returns you to revising your to-be model, after which you once again begin the process of meeting with prospects—this time with updated assumptions. When you feel ready to sell your new model, be confident. You can succeed and you will succeed in winning a **Customer**.

THE SOFTWARE TECHNICIAN

Should You Become Self-Employed?

Dennis

Dennis Shieh, a software technician for Dell, was troubled by growing job-related stress. So, when the company went through a downturn and offered early retirement packages, he accepted.

Dennis liked being a technical professional and drew up a work model based on buying and running a retail computer store. He promptly tested his new model by visiting a business broker, who recommended (1) reviewing the financials of computer stores for sale, and (2) taking a personality assessment.

Dennis did both, and learned that (1) computer stores are low-margin, high-turnover operations with poor overall profitability, and (2) he lacked a consumer-service personality—he was better off focusing on backroom technical tasks and avoiding people-handling responsibilities.

So Dennis pivoted, revamped his work model, and replaced consumers with technical business-to-business clients.

Soon an opportunity arose that Dennis would have dismissed under his initial model: a company that sold, serviced, calibrated, and certified commercial scales, from postage meters to heavy-duty devices for weighing trucks and airplanes. The firm met Dennis's needs to independently exercise technical skills, minimize contact with technically unsophisticated customers, and earn a good, independent living with minimal stress.

Dennis bought the company and now happily enjoys working as a business owner—often in shorts and a t-shirt.

When a Customer hires you —in whatever capacity—you've validated your work model. If you're an employee, you've found the key Customer you need. If you're an entrepreneur or contractor, you've acquired a new Customer. Your new work model has taken flight. Congratulations!

THE DATA ANALYST

Georg

"Disadvantage" Becomes Superpower

Julia Sammann, a Hamburg-based career consultant and coach trained in work model-ing, prides herself on guiding people along the journey to what she calls their professional "Nextland." But during her first session with Georg M., a new client, she was surprised by an unexpected confession.

"I'm autistic," said Georg. "I have Asperger's syndrome."

Asperger's was unfamiliar to Julia, though she had noticed a couple of Georg's unusual habits, such as avoiding eye contact during their session. Still, she liked Georg and was impressed with his keen intel-ligence, so she resolved not to do any background reading about the effects of Asperger's syndrome. "I thought it might bias my approach," she says.

Julia

During their second coaching session, Julia began to see how Asperger's had influenced Georg's working style, interests, and abilities. People with Asperger's all have their own per-sonality and individual characteristics, but what they often have in common are highly special-ized interests, challenges with social interaction and understanding nonverbal communica-tions—and difficulties with employment.

Yet Georg had been successfully employed as an experienced data analyst in a consulting firm, losing his job only because his employer went bankrupt. As he sought new work, Georg could find no jobs matching his personality and unique skills. He decided he wanted to start his own business instead.

As a first step toward this goal, Julia had Georg depict his as-is work model. Immediately it became clear that Georg considered Asperger's to be a severe disadvantage in his Who You Are building block:

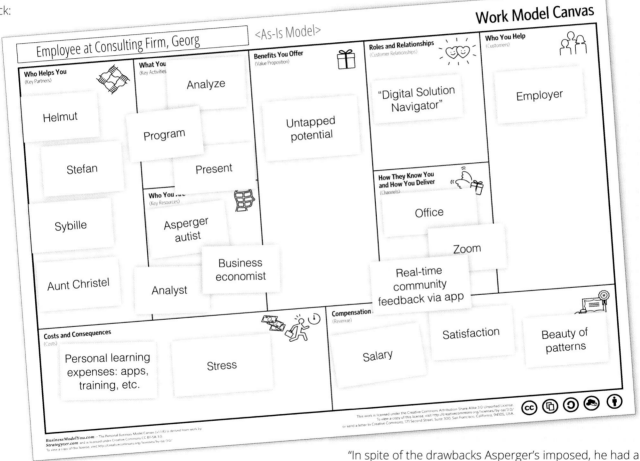

"In spite of the drawbacks Asperger's imposed, he had a diverse skill set with outstanding expertise in several areas, including data-driven decision-making," says Julia. "He quickly became one of my favorite clients."

During their next session, Julia asked Georg to define his "superpower"—and how he might "conquer the world with it." Georg claimed the ability to "design structures" as his superpower. Superpower-like abilities in mathematics, music, data analysis, or other specific domains are, in fact, often displayed by people with Asperger's syndrome. And as Julia and Georg explored his Who You Are in more depth, Georg realized that

Asperger's was indeed the very quality that fueled his exceptional ability to design frameworks for capturing and analyzing data. For the first time, Georg recognized that his autistic nature was, in fact, a secret weapon he could use to create value for clients. As he put it, "as an Asperger autist, I both need structure and give structure."

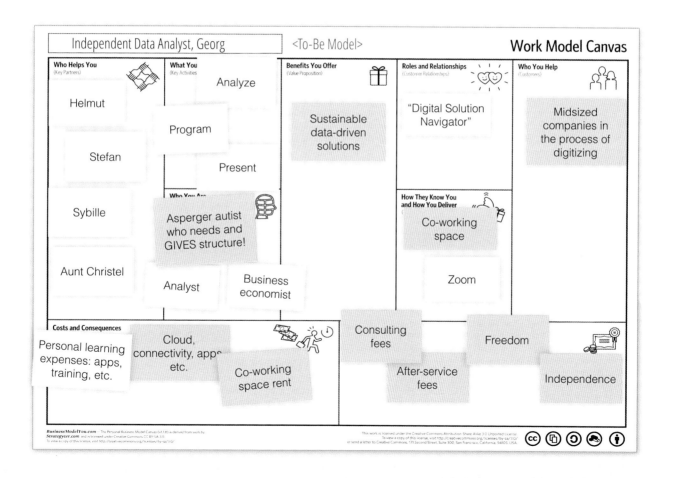

"No matter what type of work I am doing, I am at my best when I can operate within structures," says Georg. "The Work Model is ideal for someone like me. It provides a well-defined way to identify and structure my expertise."

Structure is important to people with Asperger's, who often prefer concrete, visual approaches to learning. Julia agrees that using a business or service model as a "third object" is an ideal way to coach clients or consult with organizations.

After only four sessions with Julia, Georg was able to clearly define his professional "Nextland":

"As a digital solutions navigator, I enable medium-sized companies to monetize their digital assets by structuring complex datasets and applying modern algorithms to extract their meaning."

Six weeks later, Georg won his first client.

"If you've met one person with autism, you've met one person with autism."

— Dr. Stephen Shore

Coach Yourself Now!

1. Do I understand my worth in the organization and the financial cost of replacing me?

2. Am I brave enough to withstand the discomfort of approaching new people? If not, how can I overcome my fear?

3. When testing, do I recognize the importance of reaching out to less important contacts first so I can get comfortable before reaching out to more important contacts?

4. When testing, am I merely asking questions—or sharing things that demonstrate I'm informed about Problems, Issues, Needs, and Trends that matter to the interviewee?

5. Did I follow up with interviewees to thank them and ensure they understood how valuable their input was to me? I shouldn't assume they know how helpful they were.

Now, it's time to learn a powerful way to position yourself to win more satisfying work. Get ready to create your personal brand!

CHAPTER 7

Brand and Promote Yourself

Reasons to Choose You

Everyone wants to attract more opportunities. That requires showing people reasons why they should choose us.

To accomplish this, we need to create and put forward clear and compelling promises of value, all while being perceived as trustworthy and credible. As the professional football player Steve Young once said, Perception is reality. *If you are perceived to be something, you might as well be it because that's the truth in people's minds.*

In this chapter, you'll learn to positively **influence** people to choose you. The secret to accomplishing this efficiently is personal branding. And because personal branding draws on principles of traditional branding, let's learn about the role of branding...from a bottle of wine!

What Is Branding?

In this photograph, a shopper is about to choose a bottle of wine from a retail store shelf. What attracts her to a particular bottle? Naturally, the label's design, colors, and graphics evoke certain emotions, while the vintner's story, a description of the terroir, suggestions for food pairings, alcohol level, and other elements also entice her. The price point of the bottle plays a role, too. *This bottle is exerting tremendous effort to convince a potential buyer to choose it.*

Why does each wine bottle make such effort to convince buyers to choose it?

Naturally, many bottles of wine are competing on the same shelf, so differentiation is important. But the biggest reason is that the true flavor and qualities of any particular wine are impossible to assess beforehand. The buyer must "trust" a bottle in advance.

Similar logic applies to working professionals. Often, we need to win the trust of someone who knows little—or nothing—about us. We may even need to influence that person before they have the chance to meet us. How can we do that? By creating a powerful personal brand.

A Personal Brand Supercharges Your Work Model

Not every worker needs a personal brand. But having one supercharges your work model, because it differentiates you from those who describe themselves with generic titles such as coaches, marketing consultants, project managers, or account executives. Such titles are akin to commodity categories such as corn, oil, or natural gas. Professionals who use generic titles likely do their jobs well, but they're unlikely to be perceived as differentiated, valuable, or in demand. In fact, professionals less skilled

than you may well enjoy better opportunities—and even be paid more!

Being a "generic" professional puts you in the position of having to pursue every possible opportunity by over-investing in selling-related Key Activities. But selling has a high failure rate, and nobody likes to be "sold" anything, especially when they see no immediate need for it. For example, have you ever sent someone an unsolicited resume? How did that work for you? *Consider personal branding the secret to being "bought" in advance.*

What's true for selling is also true for the opposite of branding: bragging. Many people think that personal branding means boasting about one's achievements. But does anyone really like people who brag? No. Bragging triggers negative emotions, and it fails

to help anybody differentiate themselves or be perceived as valuable and in demand.

Having a good personal brand also differs from simply having a good professional reputation. It is much more! Having a good reputation means being considered a "good" plumber, tax advisor, or account manager: it means you can be trusted to competently perform a specific task. But having a strong personal brand means being considered *exactly the right person for the job, sight unseen*. It means you are both relevant to the Customer's needs—and credible in the Customer's eyes.

Think of a personal brand as an additional Key Resource that supercharges your entire work model. On the next pages, consider how a strong personal brand strengthens other building blocks and makes your work model easier to execute.

Customers

The shared values and personality traits conveyed by your personal brand ensure that Customers self-qualify and self-select themselves for you, as shown in Cyd's case on page 166. This reduces the time, trouble, and expense of attracting and acquiring new opportunities.

Benefits You Offer

A strong personal brand clarifies and amplifies the benefits you offer, differentiating you from others and making you relevant and compelling to prospective clients. Your brand also implies emotional and social values that help people feel safer choosing you. For example, Emma, an architect and civil engineer with a deep love of gardening, became well-known in Italy's Monza province for her easy-maintenance, sustainable approach to gardens. Emma quickly became the "go to" person for villas owners eager to show off their gardens while minimizing maintenance.

Roles and Relationships

A strong personal brand can transform "push" relationships—where you must actively pursue clients—into "pull" relationships whereby you naturally attract opportunities. A good brand casts you in a desirable role: as the "go to" person in a specific field or organization. Remember Eric from page 96? Before revising his work model, internal and external clients alike considered Eric the installation expert for EPIC software. And in fact, being in such high demand triggered conflict with that role—a conflict that gave birth to a new role and a new personal brand.

Compensation and Rewards

One key benefit of a clear, strong personal brand is that you win more work that truly matters to you, which in turn brings more personal fulfillment—plus better compensation. For example, Johanna is a 31-year-old freelance German-to-English translator who lacked a personal brand strategy and grew tired of doing general-purpose translation on a fee-per-word basis. Because she has a post-graduate degree in human resource management, she branded herself as a specialist in personnel recruiting translations—and quickly won assignments from the human resource departments of two large corporations. That work proved far more rewarding to Johanna, both personally and financially.

Who Helps You

When you have a strong personal brand, people who share your values and appreciate your style want to work with you. This makes for stronger and more efficient collaborations. For example, Paola, a 36-year-old former performing artist, worked as a set designer for several subcontractors that all served a large event production firm. When she took a job with that production firm as an events director, her deep experience with its subcontractors—plus her background as an artist and set designer—made her the perfect liaison for handling her new employer's Key Partners.

Costs and Consequences

A strong personal brand reduces selling costs and avoids wasting resources on the wrong Channels. For example, the ground-breaking CEO of one of the world's largest energy companies was plagued with constant requests for interviews and events. He was delighted when his new personal brand strategy enabled his team to filter out requests to a manageable number, all of which were prequalified to focus on his core message about sustainability.

So, how do you create this powerful new Key Resource in your work model? The first step is to become aware of all the elements you can use to impress the right people: your Audience. Once you have defined your Audience, you can craft your personal brand, then devise strategies to communicate that brand to your Audience.

Here's a new visual tool specifically designed to do exactly that: the Personal Brand Canvas![19] This one-page tool, created by Luigi Centenaro when he was inspired by the first edition of *Business Model You*, includes every element needed to build your own personal brand. Start now by placing sticky notes on the Canvas. Or better yet, download a free PDF file of the **Personal Brand Canvas** at BigName.pro/BMY/ and print out an oversized version you can work on at home. Rest assured: your work model already contains much of the material you need!

Audience: Who Needs to Know

Start with the most fundamental element of your personal brand: Audience. But keep in mind that personal branding is not about being famous! It is about being *selectively famous*: known only among people who can help you reach your goals.

These people are your Audience—the people you need to influence. Typically they are customers, clients, constituents, colleagues, **Key Partners**, or other stakeholders. Your Audience may also include people who *influence* these stakeholders.

Once you've defined your Audience, it's time to create the secret levers that power your personal brand. Start by focusing on the big circle on the left that represents...you! It includes four important building blocks: Profession, Competence, Identity, and Reasons to Believe.

 ### Profession: *What You Do and How You Do It*

If you want to brand your *current* role, fill in the Profession building block based on your current role. If you seek a *new or different role*, fill in the Profession building block based on your *desired* role. In either case, describe your Profession as clearly as you can. Include your job title, role, and specific responsibilities.

Next, describe specifically how you do your job. This is your professional approach, the very essence of your work model—as you would introduce it to somebody else. For example, within your specialty you might use a particular methodology, or apply a multidisciplinary skill set. It's fine to describe yourself using words such as "innovative" or "unconventional." But if you do, be sure to explain specifically how you are innovative or unconventional. Remember when Georg rebranded himself as a "digital solutions navigator" in the case on page 175? His new role was to enable medium-sized companies to monetize their digital assets using this specific approach: *structuring complex datasets and applying modern algorithms to extract their meaning.*

Some people struggle with describing their professions. For one, their employers may use vague or confusing job titles, or even lack a coherent job title policy. If you have trouble writing a job title readily understandable by your Audience, just briefly explain your role using simple terms. People who go through this exercise often end up proposing more effective new job titles to their managers!

The Personal Brand Canvas

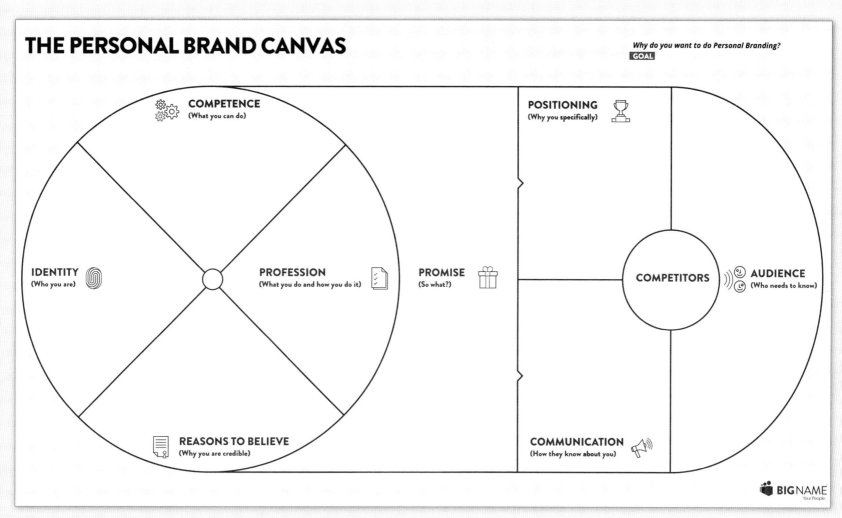

THE PERSONAL BRAND CANVAS

Why do you want to do Personal Branding?
GOAL

COMPETENCE
(What you can do)

POSITIONING
(Why you specifically)

IDENTITY
(Who you are)

PROFESSION
(What you do and how you do it)

PROMISE
(So what?)

COMPETITORS

AUDIENCE
(Who needs to know)

REASONS TO BELIEVE
(Why you are credible)

COMMUNICATION
(How they know about you)

BIGNAME
Your People.

Download the Personal Brand Canvas here: **BigName.Pro/BMY**

Competence: What You Can Do

Now it's time to showcase your Competence. In the Competence block, list what is truly important and relevant to your Audience. Competence can include elements from the Key Resources block in your work model, such as skills, abilities, training, and domain knowledge related to your Profession. Be specific and keep it on a need-to-know basis: list only those elements that will positively impress your Audience. Leave out generic or secondary competencies such as "strong empathy," "good listener," or "Excel expertise" *unless they are specifically required for your role—and your credibility regarding the competency is high.*

Discerning the most relevant elements in your Competence block can be difficult. An excellent exercise for becoming aware of your competencies is the Lifeline Discovery explained on pages 120–123. Online assessment tools such as StrengthsFinder can be useful as well. Or visit ONetOnline.org, pull down the Advanced Search menu, and review the knowledge, skill, and ability definitions.

Identity: Who You Are

Identity may well be the most important element in your personal branding strategy: it defines what makes you special in your Audience's eyes and differentiates you from others who do similar work. The Identity block is also where you project likability and empathy. Bear in mind that *personal brands are rooted in authenticity.* Authenticity is essential, not only for obvious ethical reasons, but because it helps you avoid the Costs and Consequences of attracting the wrong opportunities.

For example, Angela, a recent graduate in finance with an outstanding academic record, played it safe by describing herself in her resume as having a "huge passion for accounting." She easily landed a job with a commercial bank, but within months realized she had ignored her strong interest in the gaming sector in favor of landing a "safe" job. She subsequently attended a personal branding workshop and joked to the trainer that "not being accountable to myself was a dumb accounting move for an accountant!"

Some downplay the importance of authenticity, thinking to themselves, *My personal values don't necessarily have to align with my business role, right?* Wrong! Trying to conceal your true Identity is more dangerous than ever: in a digitally overconnected world, the truth is mere clicks away, waiting to be uncovered by anyone.

What's more, authenticity is essential for connecting with people emotionally and building loyalty. As the saying goes, *Like attracts like:* we are attracted to people who are similar to us. The more explicitly authentic you are when communicating, the more common ground you will build with your Audience. This applies whether you need to attract new opportunities by impressing people who don't know you yet or change the perception of people who already know you. **We all admire and prefer to deal with people who are competent, but what we value first and foremost in people is trustworthiness—which is gained by being authentic.**

So, list elements such as personality traits, cultural heritage, values, and interests: these will sharpen your Identity and boost your authenticity. Some of these elements may already be in the Key Resources block of your work model.

Consider, too, that we tend to like people who cooperate with us toward mutual goals. So, list your ambitions, convictions, and causes you believe in or support. Similarly, we are also defined by what we don't like—by our adversaries. *The enemy of my enemy*

> *"The most exhausting thing you can be is inauthentic."*
>
> — Anne Morrow Lindbergh

is my friend, as the saying goes. So, consider adding something about your idiosyncrasies, dislikes, or people or ideas you oppose—your personal crusades.

But your two main energy sources for inspiring other people are the following:

First, professional perspective. Can you articulate how you see the future of your profession or industry? Future vision is a source of thought leadership. People prefer to deal with those who possess an interesting professional perspective.

Second, purpose. What is your purpose? What ultimately drives your actions and powers your work model? As detailed in Simon Sinek's bestseller *Start With Why*, people are less inspired by *what* you do, and more by *why* you do it. For example, Milena, a wealth advisor for a large Italian bank, specializes in the needs of successful women entrepreneurs. Milena's approach, captured in her "less finance, more life plans" motto, is to use financial education and planning to help such women become independent in their financial lives.

Reasons to Believe: What Makes You Credible?

Time to focus on the next block: Reasons to Believe. In other words, show them the

evidence! This block is where you establish credibility and generate trust. As Robert Cialdini has persuasively shown, people look to the behavior of others to determine their own actions, especially when they feel uncertain. They tend to follow the lead of credible, knowledgeable experts.

This means you should select and list provable facts, such as professional experience, work portfolio, professional results, job titles obtained or awards won, testimonials or endorsements from noteworthy professionals, diplomas, academic roles or recognition, certifications, internships, membership in associations, volunteer work, nationality (if relevant), experience abroad, publications, and so forth. Emilio, a 54-year-old real estate agent from Sorrento, uses a surprising talking point to establish credibility in a sector notorious for part-time agents who constantly enter and leave the industry. "I've had the same mobile telephone number since 1997," he says.

Promise: So What?

You've defined the levers that activate your personal brand. Now it's time to define your promise to your Audience: your promise to deliver value.

Think of Starbucks or McDonald's. Whether you are a fan of these brands or not, as soon

as you see their iconic logos, you know exactly what these companies promise and the benefits you will enjoy when dealing with them. This is true even if you have never entered a Starbucks or McDonald's! Similarly, your job as a one-person brand is to ensure people in your Audience can clearly picture your Promise of value and find it meaningful and important. Your Promise tells them you are the person who will get the job done.

Be explicit about your Promise. Add to this block every element from your work model's Value Proposition—Benefits You Offer—that are relevant to your Audience. Think, too, in terms of emotional and social benefits. Include any other valuable reasons why they should choose you. For example, Jessica was a 28-year-old social media manager working in a modern, digital-savvy fashion company in Paris. She became quite influential online, and ended up being hired away by another, more traditional fashion house whose brand needed rejuvenating. Jessica's new employer wanted to be perceived by young people as an ideal place to work, and they highly appraised Jessica's capacity to serve as a youthful, savvy, and purposeful amplifier of their brand.

Let's move to the right side of the Brand Canvas, specifically to Positioning (your differentiation) and Communication (the way you engage your Audience). These building blocks enable you to design specific branding actions. To get started, first describe your competitors.

Competitors

Many workers believe they have no competitors. This belief is common; such workers concentrate on themselves and pay little attention to other people. But most likely your Audience is paying attention to other people! Everybody faces competition, whether it comes from someone exiting your boss or client's office—or the office of a hiring manager just before it's your turn to interview!

Who are your competitors? They are people actively trying to win the same kinds of opportunities as you, or who are trying to influence and impress the same Audience as you. This is why the Competitor block stands between the Audience and Positioning blocks on the Personal Brand Canvas.

List your biggest rivals in the Competitors block. If you can't find specific names, simply write down appropriate job titles or roles. A good exercise is to study LinkedIn® or other social networking services or personal websites to understand how people doing similar work differ from you.

Positioning: Why You Specifically

Now it's time to ensure you are remarkable and stand out from the crowd by defining the Positioning block of your personal brand.

The key question to answer here is, Why you specifically? Why should people in your Audience choose you over your Competitors? Will you be part of the background noise, or will you be remarkable and stand apart from the crowd? Positioning relates to how you differentiate yourself from others, from your Competitors, and indeed how you are perceived in the minds of your Audience compared to others.

Many people working with the Personal Brand Canvas for the first time struggle with Positioning. Rather than listing points of difference, they start with listing points of parity: areas where they are equivalent to Competitors. They have a natural tendency to list elements that place them in "the middle of the pack," so to speak. This positioning feels safe—like a place from which they can grab the most opportunities.

But this middle-of-the-road approach contradicts the relevancy demanded by Customers who seek something that precisely addresses an important need.

One common mistake is the "one-man band" approach: I can do a bit of everything. But as the saying goes, a little knowledge is dangerous. When we position ourselves as being good at many things, in fact we convey the impression of not being truly skilled at anything. And even if we are, in fact, good at many things, from an Audience standpoint it still sounds too good to be true. But it is a different thing altogether to offer specific, credible, multidisciplinary solutions to accomplish jobs faster, better, or more efficiently.

Another common mistake is promoting "passion" as a differentiation—as if competitors would introduce themselves as not being passionate! Other generic, middle-of-the-road descriptors that fail to position you effectively include "empathy," "good listener," "team player," and the like.

The good news is that your most potent differentiators should already be listed in other Canvas blocks. If you have compiled your Canvas properly, you simply need to choose the most relevant, credible, and important elements from one of the seven building blocks on the next page.

Before moving to the Communication block, let's consider the case of a professional who used the Personal Brand Canvas for the first time.

IDENTITY
(Who you are)

Show what makes you truly stand out in the eyes of your Audience—including the special, inspirational ideas you believe in that influence everything you do. Examples include your purpose, your professional perspective, and your unique heritage and history.

COMPETENCE
(What you can do)

Explain what you know or can do particularly well.

PROFESSION
(What you do and how you do it)

Detail your unique professional approach and/or the distinctive aspects of what you do.

REASONS TO BELIEVE
(Why you are credible)

Describe specific experiences, credentials, facts, technologies, or assets you possess or use that make you credible.

PROMISE
(So what?)

List the specific benefits you provide that set you apart from the crowd.

AUDIENCE
(Who needs to know)

The industry, people, or specific organizations you focus on.

Mariam

Mariam's First Canvas: Weak Promise, Positioning

Mariam, an American born in Bulgaria, is a 36-year-old senior project manager with ten years of experience working in an international government-supported agency that focuses on social services innovation.

Mariam fell in love with design thinking methodologies after participating in some related bootcamps and self-study courses, then applying what she learned in two agency projects.

But those and other projects failed to gain real traction, and Mariam started feeling discouraged by the slow progress and never-ending compromises required in the international social services sector.

Meanwhile, she grew excited about the idea of working as a strategy designer for a high-flying design agency such as Ideo or Frog Design. Her first Personal Brand Canvas, aimed at securing a strategist position with such an agency, appears on the opposite page.

Keep reading to learn how Mariam—and you—can rework your initial Canvas to create a powerful personal brand!

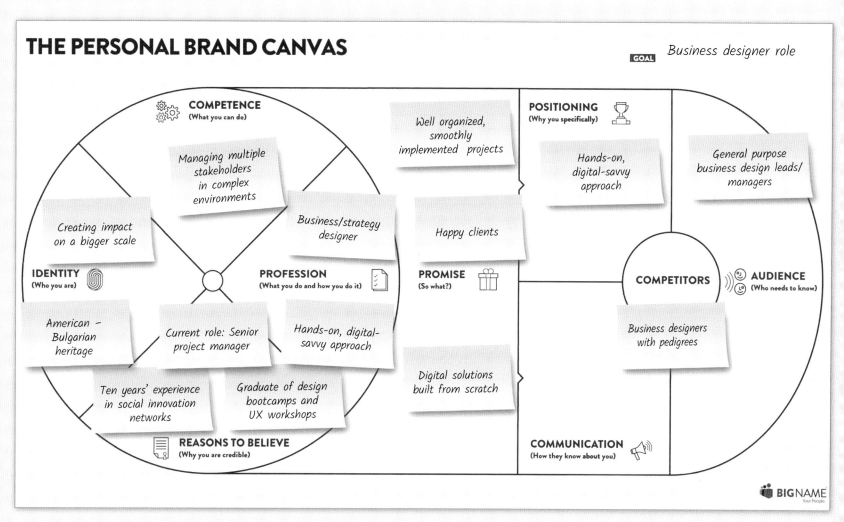

THE PERSONAL BRAND CANVAS

GOAL *Business designer role*

COMPETENCE
(What you can do)

Managing multiple stakeholders in complex environments

Creating impact on a bigger scale

IDENTITY
(Who you are)

American – Bulgarian heritage

PROFESSION
(What you do and how you do it)

Business/strategy designer

Current role: Senior project manager

Hands-on, digital-savvy approach

Ten years' experience in social innovation networks

Graduate of design bootcamps and UX workshops

REASONS TO BELIEVE
(Why you are credible)

Well organized, smoothly implemented projects

Happy clients

PROMISE
(So what?)

Digital solutions built from scratch

POSITIONING
(Why you specifically)

Hands-on, digital-savvy approach

General purpose business design leads/ managers

COMPETITORS

Business designers with pedigrees

AUDIENCE
(Who needs to know)

COMMUNICATION
(How they know about you)

BIGNAME
Your People.

Download the Personal Brand Canvas here: **BigName.Pro/BMY**

How to Solve Personal Brand Canvas Problems

Here are some common problems faced when working on a Personal Brand Canvas—and how to solve them.

You Struggle Filling in Blocks

You may find yourself struggling to fill in your Profession or Identity details, or you may realize you need new or better Reasons to Believe or Competencies. This is normal. Design is struggling—and struggling is design! You may need to review or re-diagram your work model or take some professional development courses. One powerful way to uncover competencies you never knew you possessed is to ask current or former colleagues for feedback on how they perceive you, as Ellen's case describes on page 108.

You Feel Like You Are Bragging

People often feel like they are bragging when they start working on a Personal Brand Canvas. But bear in mind that the Canvas, like other third objects, is simply a tool for ideating—it's not something you show to your Audience. It's designed to provoke you to dig deeper and articulate insights about yourself. Think of it as an "internal use only" blueprint for your personal branding strategy. Your goal in building a Canvas is to achieve clarity, connect the dots, and generate new options for yourself. Afterwards you will design indirect and more elegant ways to communicate your personal brand to your Audience.

Too Many Sticky Notes?

You might worry about ending up with too many sticky notes. Don't! Think of your first work with the Canvas as brainstorming. Later, you can easily remove elements that are redundant, confusing, or of minor importance. The key is to keep a sharp focus on those elements your Audience truly needs to know about. Your decision criterion is very simple: *Does an element contribute to generating a strong Promise? If not, remove it. Don't waste your time—or your Audience's time!*

Unsatisfied With Your Promise?

If you're unsatisfied with your Promise, try "squeezing" it. You "squeeze" your Promise by asking the following question, preferably with a thought partner who can provide objectivity and a fresh perspective:

What impression will I make—and what sort of value will my Audience perceive—when they see elements of my Identity, Competence, or Reasons to Believe?

Add to your Promise block any new elements that emerge from this "squeeze" thought experiment.

Personal Brand Fitness

When you have completed the first full draft of your Personal Brand Canvas, you will have identified elements that, when properly communicated to your Audience, will convey your Promise. But how can you be sure your personal brand will prove effective? You'll soon discover that designing and activating your personal brand also means testing your work model. That's when it's time for some personal brand fitness!

The Fit Test

The first test is to ensure you are a good fit. Every Profession has specific requirements, meaning your Audience expects certain elements when evaluating you. Without these elements, you are unqualified even to converse with your Audience. You have no chance to differentiate yourself: you are like a bottle of wine sitting on the laundry soap shelf! Trying to change your Audience's expectations about what's required for a specific job is the worst gravity problem you could ever face—so don't try to do it.

For example, one MBA student with no fashion sector experience told the school's head of career services that upon graduation she wanted to enter Italy's notoriously exclusive high fashion industry. The reply was blunt: *If you are not part of the Italian fashion industry, you will not be hired by the Italian fashion industry.*

Try answering these questions:

1. Do you fit? Do you meet all the requirements (Competence, Reasons to Believe, and Identity) for your intended Profession?

2. Can you offer benefits to Customers? Is your Promise relevant to what your Audience needs or desires? Have you verified this using the PINT tool discussed on page 160 and the model testing processes explained on pages 164–173?

3. Are your Identity elements inspiring and meaningful to your Audience? If not, either (1) develop the required elements, or (2) change your Audience.

4. Do you need more information about the Profession and its requirements? If so, examine competitor profiles and job postings on services such as LinkedIn®. If you don't respect the profession's requirements, you're not even in the game.

Want More Credibility? Mine Your Memory

Serena served as the digital communications manager for a large airport in Italy, where she had sought an internal promotion without success. She started working on a Personal Brand Canvas so she could apply for a position as head of communications for a large healthcare provider.

"My first version of the Canvas completely left out the fact that for two years I managed a multidisciplinary team dealing with both institutional and COVID-related communications," she says. "That work had significant reputational and brand impact on our organization—and a lot of regulatory constraints were involved. But this only came out when I did the Lifeline Discovery exercise!"

Serena "mined" her memory to uncover a tangible experience that significantly strengthened her credibility for the healthcare position. She discovered that Reasons to Believe often hide in the depths of memory. And the best exercise for uncovering them is the Lifeline Discovery. You can do the same. See page 120.

Eric had a similar experience, as described on page 156. He did not feel credible as a traditional trainer, and his first training session fell flat because he made the tactical mistake of trying to behave like a traditional trainer instead of acting authentically and leveraging his true positioning. His supervisor reminded him that he had very significant experience informally training hospital IT managers. Once he adopted a natural approach, his training became effective and his new brand credible to his Audience of junior system engineers.

Sometimes, though, you simply lack Reasons to Believe, meaning you must create Reasons from scratch. One way is to earn new credentials or certifications. If this would incur excessive hard or soft costs, you might enroll in self-study courses or take on pro bono or volunteer projects to gain experience in specific areas.

Consistency Check

The idea here is to check whether your Promise is consistent with what you describe in your Profession, Competence, Reasons to Believe, and Identity building blocks.

For example, Stephanie, a European patent attorney with an electrical engineering background, wanted potential clients (her Audience) to understand that she offers "ready-to-apply technical workarounds" (her Promise). But in the first version of her Personal Brand Canvas, she neglected to mention specific mechatronics engineering expertise that enables her to offer both customized consulting and alternative technical solution services for difficult-to-patent inventions. She revised her Canvas to make her Promise consistent with the other building blocks: "Custom consulting and technical solution services for difficult-to-patent inventions."

Positioning test

Franco, a 42-year-old project manager in the oil and gas industry, was complaining to his new branding coach.

"I've been looking for a job in my field for a while but haven't even been called for interviews. It's very strange—I'm very experienced in this field."

"No doubt you're experienced, but much depends on how you differentiate yourself against others—your competitors," came the reply.

"But I'm not a freelancer, so I don't have competitors. We're all very similar in my field, anyway. So it's not really possible to differentiate," Franco insisted.

The coach smiled patiently. He had heard statements like Franco's many times before.

"Your competitors are those who applied for the same jobs and got called for interviews. Maybe they didn't get hired, but at least they got on a shortlist and had the chance to interview and play their best cards. They stood out from the background noise: their profiles were noticed for good reasons."

As the two continued working on Franco's Personal Brand Canvas, it emerged that Franco had managed two important sustainability-related projects during the previous three years. He incorporated insights from this powerful experience into the next iteration of his Canvas.

Key Questions to Ask Yourself
— Is your Positioning strong enough to set you apart from competitors?
— Is your Positioning hard to copy?
— Does your Positioning create enough opportunities?

Mariam's Revised Canvas: Strong Promise & Positioning

Mariam—from page 192—sounded confident and excited about her first Canvas iteration, but a professional branding coach suggested she validate her strategy through interviews and analysis of LinkedIn® job postings. That led her to realize her Positioning was weak and she was a poor fit for design agencies that typically require strong formal design backgrounds when hiring. She also saw that her Promise was insufficiently relevant to the design agency Audience.

Thanks to these discoveries, Mariam learned about Certified B Corporations—for-profit entities certified as being socially responsible and transparent—and the consulting firms and agencies that serve them.

Meanwhile, while conducting the Lifeline Discovery exercise with her coach, she had an epiphany. For the first time, she realized that as a project manager she had not only sought out, secured, and managed project stakeholders, but in fact she had devised, designed, and developed projects from scratch: from conception to funding to execution.

As a result, Mariam decided to change her Audience to consultancy firms and agencies that serve Certified B Corporations. This was a more logical and compelling Audience, given both her network and her relevant, highly credible experience in social innovation.

After revising her Personal Brand Canvas as per the opposite page, she started networking with people in her new target Audience and writing content on LinkedIn® about the relationship between design thinking, social innovation, and large project stakeholder management. This resulted in her winning a temporary job in an incubator-like facility dedicated to serving Certified B Corporations.

Mariam

THE PERSONAL BRAND CANVAS

GOAL *Business designer role*

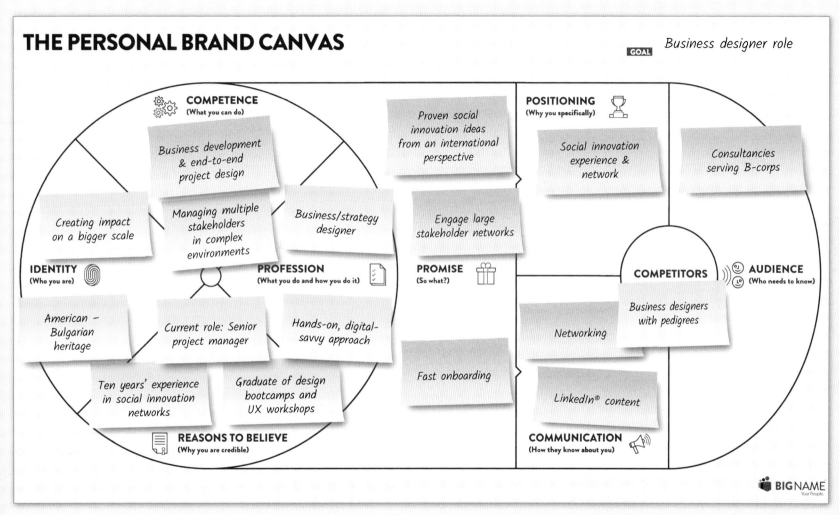

COMPETENCE
(What you can do)

Business development & end-to-end project design

Managing multiple stakeholders in complex environments

Business/strategy designer

Creating impact on a bigger scale

IDENTITY
(Who you are)

American – Bulgarian heritage

Current role: Senior project manager

Hands-on, digital-savvy approach

PROFESSION
(What you do and how you do it)

Ten years' experience in social innovation networks

Graduate of design bootcamps and UX workshops

REASONS TO BELIEVE
(Why you are credible)

Proven social innovation ideas from an international perspective

Engage large stakeholder networks

PROMISE
(So what?)

Fast onboarding

POSITIONING
(Why you specifically)

Social innovation experience & network

Consultancies serving B-corps

COMPETITORS

Business designers with pedigrees

AUDIENCE
(Who needs to know)

Networking

LinkedIn® content

COMMUNICATION
(How they know about you)

BIGNAME
Your People.

Download the Personal Brand Canvas here: **BigName.Pro/BMY**

How to Engage Your Audience

As Mariam's experience shows, the Personal Brand Canvas helps validate your overall work model—in fact, your personal brand is inseparable from that model. The more you interview relevant stakeholders, the more efficient this validation process becomes, and the more clearly your Audience perceives you. Remember, you are not selling while validating your model. Don't feel disappointed if interviewees fail to show immediate interest. You are seeking feedback and perceptions, not a "sale."

Once you have validated your work model, it is time to proactively engage your Audience and grow your personal brand. Engaging your Audience means ensuring that (1) your Promise and Positioning are clear in the Audience's mind, and (2) the key elements in your Personal Brand Canvas are easily discoverable and/or known by your Audience. How do you do this?

First, by introducing yourself in the clearest, most persuasive way possible. Next, by designing communications or creating interactions to let your Audience grasp your value beforehand and become inspired to "buy." Yes, like a bottle of wine!

Consistency is the key. The way you introduce yourself or engage with your Audience must be consistent with the sticky notes on your Personal Brand Canvas. The most readily accessible way to introduce yourself is, of course, through online profiles on LinkedIn® or other social media services—more about that in a moment. But first, let's examine an important truth about first impressions—and trust.

Warmth Beats Competence

What creates a positive impression when you meet someone for the first time? Social psychologist Amy Cuddy has a surprising answer to that question.

It turns out that two traits—warmth and competence—account for 80 to 90% of overall first impressions. This finding holds true across cultures. But which trait is more important?

Many people are surprised to learn that *warmth is more important than competence*.

Why? Because when we meet someone for the first time, we subconsciously answer two questions: *What are this person's intentions toward me?* and *How competent is this person?*

Our subconscious answer to the question about intention determines whether we believe the person is trustworthy—*and that answer is determined by the person's warmth*. Our subconscious answer to the question about competence determines whether we believe the person is *capable of enacting their intentions*. If we perceive them as untrustworthy but competent, we'll grow cautious—we might even perceive them as an adversary.

The point is that warmth is not only perceived first, but it accounts for more of the overall first impression than competence. Note the diagram showing how we *admire* people who are warm and competent, *pity* those who are warm but incompetent, *envy* those who are cold but competent, and *dislike* those who are cold and incompetent.

	Competent	Incompetent
Warm	**Admiration** is inspired by warm competence	**Pity** is invoked by warm incompetence
Cold	**Envy** is invited by cold competence	**Contempt** is aroused by cold incompetence

Warmth lives in your Identity block. This is why it is so important to express your personality traits, personal heritage, values, interests, idiosyncrasies, and other elements in this part of your Personal Brand Canvas. Make sure you project both warmth and competence!

📢 Communication: How They Know About You

This is where you add sticky notes describing specific communications that convey your brand to your Audience. We recommend working with a thought partner to do this: find another reader of this book and help each other build your respective personal brands.

First, Craft a Digital Identity That Doesn't Suck

First impressions are often created online, especially among professionals engaged in intellectual work. Digital media offers multiple touchpoints that can directly access Audiences and the opportunities they represent.

Still, many people remain more concerned with how their physical world presence affects their professional image and fail to think of digital interactions as "real." This is why instant messaging profiles often feature poor-quality descriptions or pictures that do not truly represent a person, even when these symbols are related to their professional identity. The same is true for online meeting platforms where it's unclear whether the person is present because they are represented by a disabled camera, funny nickname—even an animal photo!

Nevertheless, today Google serves as your default resume or CV—and Google plays close attention to professional and personal social networking profile pages. Search your name on Google, and it is quite possible your LinkedIn® profile will appear as one of the first search results.

Therefore, introducing yourself correctly online is key. It is not a question of being polished, fashionable, or showing off a certain lifestyle. The goal is to be authentic and in charge of your professional image. Use your online introduction to attract and influence other people. Think of digital tools as outsourced marketing robots constantly working on your behalf, striving to introduce you to your Audience. This is where your Personal Brand Canvas will prove extremely useful. For example, consider the following recommendations for your LinkedIn® profile.

Photograph

Start with a digital photograph of yourself. Your photo functions just like an organization's logo. Aside from your name, it's the most visual element in your profile and therefore the most memorable. Make sure your photograph is taken professionally and captures key elements of your Identity and Positioning. Share your Canvas with the photographer: photographers are trained to choose the right background, lighting, and pose to communicate a desired image. Use this same professional photograph for all digital tools, profiles, and touchpoints.

Headline Section

In your LinkedIn® "headline" definition of who you are or what you do, combine elements of your Profession and Positioning blocks as concisely as possible. When you can, add keywords reflecting key elements of your Identity. Another option is to feature a concise statement combining your Promise and Identity.

About Section

Introduce yourself as if you were standing in front of the reader. Start by describing your Profession and Positioning in more detail. Use the first-person voice to speak directly to the reader in a tone that matches your Identity—your values and personality. If applicable, indicate exactly how you can help members of your Audience—what you Promise them. Then list some relevant Competence elements, whenever possible aligning them with facts from your Reasons to Believe block. Remember, establishing trust is crucial. Finish with significant elements of your Identity: this is where you create empathy with your Audience.

Remember that digital media give others the opportunity to sample your Promise. The digital ecosystem enables you to easily develop initiatives in the form of newsletters, online events, or communities, whether open to the public or internally for your own organization. Social media let you publish content or launch initiatives that demonstrate your domain competence. Just about any sticky note on your Personal Brand Canvas can serve as a source of good content. For example:

1. Share a story about an event you organized or participated in that relates to your Competence, Positioning, or Reasons to Believe.
2. Describe something new you learned that strengthens your Competence or aligns with your Positioning.
3. Summarize the latest article or book you read that aligns with your Competence or Positioning.
4. Comment in line with your Positioning on articles, essays, or books written by experts or others in your field who serve as proxies for your Audience.

Your communications need not be limited to online media. Brainstorm with a thought partner about off-line initiatives through which you can promote your new personal brand: seminars, speaking engagements, presentations at networking events, membership in professional groups such as Toastmasters, pro bono or other volunteer work done in a professional capacity, teaching a class—these and more can serve as potentially powerful Channels through which to communicate your personal brand.

Here's a tip: consider joining a professional organization *where you are unlike the other professionals in the room.* If you can make yourself relevant to this Audience, you'll be positioned as unique and interesting. For example, John, a 58-year-old career coach, joined a local association of management consultants. His trustworthy, competent self-presentation soon found half the members referring their spouses to him for career help.

As another example, Giovanni is a 37-year old banker who was struggling to Move Up into a role as a financial advisor. In particular, he wanted to attract more entrepreneurs as customers. But he faced a tough problem.

"I have fiduciary and ethical responsibilities—my client names and financial results are confidential," Giovanni explained. "How can I generate support for my Promise? I can't tell other people, *My client Lorenzo doubled his firm's value by taking my advice!*"

"But *Lorenzo* can tell other people," his thought partner replied. "Why don't you organize an educational event involving some of your most loyal and important clients?"

Giovanni ended up organizing a seminar where his best clients spoke about their successes using his bank's alternative financing services.

Coach Yourself Now!

 Do I describe myself like a commodity? Or am I perceived as differentiated and in-demand?

 Am I over-investing in selling by chasing every opportunity? Have I researched how competitors do things differently?

 Is my communication over-focused on Competence? Or does my Identity block project warmth, which is even more important than Competence?

Is my work model credible? Have I tested it with potential Audience members as described on pages 164–173?

 Do I have a strong, thematically unified digital profile? Am I proactively treating digital tools and services as marketing "robots" that help build my personal brand?

In the next chapters you'll discover how to use Outward Focus, Modeling, and the Three Questions to ensure your work model *sends* you somewhere rather than *keeps* you somewhere!

Next Steps

CHAPTER 8

The Three Commandments of Career Change

Bedrock Principles for a Distracted World

This book presents a method for reinventing how you work. The method's power has been demonstrated from a decade of teaching, training, coaching, and consulting work with thousands of people worldwide, from students to retirees, and with dozens of organizations, from small family firms to global conglomerates employing 50,000 or more. Now, these final chapters show you how to use the method to manage your career going forward.

People in every era believe they live in turbulent times, but today's turbulence coincides with unprecedented digital distraction. So, in this distracted world it can be both useful and comforting to recognize bedrock principles of work described on page 19, the most important of which is **the essence of work is service: service to basic human needs.**

Managing your career along these bedrock principles is made easier by what we call the Three Commandments of Career Change, which appear throughout the book. Whenever you face a workplace problem or find yourself agonizing over your next career move, try applying one or more of the Three Commandments: (1) Keep Outward Focus, (2) Model, and (3) When in Doubt, Ask the Three Questions.

1. Keep Outward Focus

Outward Focus means seeing beyond your own tasks and grasping how your actions affect others—and how their actions affect you. It means recognizing workplace interdependencies and behaving so you serve the entire team or enterprise. Alan's story on page 46 provides a simple example of Outward Focus. Alan's supervisor recommended that Alan ask himself two questions before undertaking any task: **(1) What can I do now to help the people who work before me and after me? and (2) How can I assist with the processes that precede and follow my work?**[20]

Use Outward Focus to think about external Customers, too. Take another look at page 19 and decide what timeless human need your work serves. If your work's connection to a basic human need is weak or indirect, consider making a change.

Finally, use Outward Focus to think about your profession. Referring to the tree metaphor on page 19, would you say your work has the qualities of a leaf, branch, trunk, or roots?

If your work is like a leaf—**a job**—expand your vision outward to the more durable **branch: your organization.** What unchanging human need does your organization serve? How do your colleagues (your Key Partners) serve that need? Do you feel pride in what your organization does? What problems, issues, needs, or trends (PINT) does your organization face? How could you help your organization address one PINT element?

If your work feels trapped on an uncomfortable **branch**—a particular **organization**—expand your vision outward to the more sustainable **trunks: industries.** Which industry serves a human need in which you have keen interest? What problems, issues, needs, or trends does that industry struggle with? What PINT element might you help that industry address from within a different organization or in a different role?

If your work feels uncomfortably positioned in a particular **industry—a trunk**—expand your vision outward to the most durable **roots: professions.** What is your preferred profession? Professionals such as accountants, biologists, and carpenters can contribute in many different organizations and industries. Are you in a good role, organization, and industry from which to contribute to your chosen profession?

2. *Model*

While this book focuses on individual work models, sketching team or enterprise models will prove extraordinarily useful throughout your lifetime. Whenever you sense a need for career change, start by modeling where you work now—or want to work in the future. Incidentally, modeling teams and enterprises is an excellent way to achieve Outward Focus. Here are ways to use modeling at three different career stages:

Early or "Encore" Career

If you are just starting your career or pursuing a new or post-retirement "encore" career, one helpful way to proceed is to identify organizations that spark your interest. Browse job listings that identify employers by name and jot down the most interesting ones. Then, pick the most intriguing employer and try diagramming its business or service model. Make educated guesses about its Customers, Value Proposition(s), Key Activities, and how it earns income (check its website for help).

Next, imagine where you might fit into that model. Put a sticky note in the building block that best "contains" the work you have in mind. For example, if you see yourself doing customer support for a software-as-a-service provider such as Salesforce.com, you'd most likely fit into the **Key Activities** building block of that organization's business model. A role in accounting at Salesforce.com, on the other hand, would put you in the **Key Resources** block, because internal accounting people do not directly deliver Salesforce.com's Value Proposition. This exercise will deepen your understanding of the organization—and how you can contribute to it.

Then, assume you work for the employer in the role you chose above, and diagram your individual work model based on that assumption. Use your new understanding of the organization (which may contain multiple assumptions) to inform your work model. Build a "story" around how you contribute to your employer's success.

You could then apply for the job advertised. But review the cautions on page 159: you'll do far better to demonstrate your initiative by approaching the organization with your own ideas about how you can contribute. Consider using some of the techniques explained on page 167 to set up an informational interview with someone who already works there.

Keep in mind that it is common for early career professionals to focus on **Key Resources** such as skills, abilities, and educational credentials and **Key Activities** related to these elements. As you progress, use Outward Focus to relate those **Resources** and **Activities** to benefits you provide.

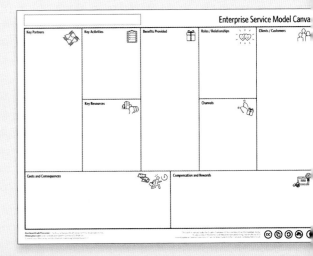

This was the case for Rami. After graduating, he spent three years in a product design firm, progressing to a level where he could directly deal with clients, who said they felt reassured by Rami's accurate listening skills. Those benefits extended to the firm, which started relying on Rami to fill in as a design team member when a firm partner was unavailable.

Midcareer

"Midcareer" differs among professions: midcareer for professional athletes might arrive at age 29, while a heart surgeon may not reach midcareer until age 45 or 50. In any case, midcareer usually means a person has developed into a domain expert or manager

and certain elements of their work model have gained greater importance. For example, interdependencies become more critical as midcareer professionals provide expertise or leadership for more complex work requiring greater collaboration with **Key Partners**. As you progress in your career, periodically update your Who Helps You block: these people can point you toward new opportunities.

Emerging elements of a midcareer work model may require different teams or organizational conditions. For example, while working as a senior developer in a nine-person boutique web development firm, Andre volunteered for a year-long community organizing project, an experience that confirmed both his leadership skills and the satisfaction he found in leading others. When the project ended, Andre realized his small employer could never offer such opportunities to develop his leadership capacity. He realized it was time to move out to a larger organization that would make this possible.

Note that your **Who You Are** block may extend beyond skills and credentials to include a reputation and personal brand that must be sustained and protected. For example, Carlita was reluctant to leave the City Water Bureau after 15 years but felt an acute need to move into a different role. Her reputation for exceptional problem solving and diplomacy had become a key element in her Who You Are building block, but low productivity and customer complaints had damaged the bureau's reputation and created a prominent pain point in the **Costs and Consequences** block of her work model. To improve the bureau's reputation and protect her own, she proposed creating and serving in a new role as a "bureau ombudswoman" who would investigate and respond to customer complaints.

Work Model Canvas

Late-Career or Retirement

Late-career professionals often enjoy a reputation for contributions made as an expert or leader. Ideally, they recognize their limitations as well as their strengths, and feel more gratitude for their successes than ambition to impress others with greater achievements. They often develop an acute awareness of how their work serves basic human needs as their focus shifts away from making money to making meaning or making expression. For a refreshed perspective on work, review the three things you can "make" on page 116.

At this career stage generativity—a concern for the future expressed in the desire to nurture and guide younger people—often emerges as a strong motivator. Late-career professionals often see generativity emerge in their work models in these ways:

- Roles and Relationships change from "expert" to "mentor" or "coach"
- Compensation and Rewards shift away from material elements and toward "soft" elements such as social contribution
- Who You Help focuses more on junior colleagues or younger Customers
- The Who Helps You block contains a long list of partners who can now be introduced to others as Key Resources

Late-career professionals may discover that Customers and Compensation change and Key Activities become less rigorous. But meaningful work and contribution can remain. Retirement usually calls for a new work model.

For example, Anthony, the hard-charging 68-year-old CEO of a successful biotech company, retired after decades of leading his firm. He joined the board of directors of a nearby medical center where he believed he could use his leadership skills to benefit hospital operations. After a few frustrating board meetings, Anaka, a board colleague, took him aside for a coaching conversation.

"Anthony, I think you'll enjoy your work on the board if you realize how it differs from your previous role as CEO. You're no longer an executive who makes key decisions and assigns responsibilities. You're an advisor to executives. You can't push them to make decisions or execute. You need to operate under a different work model in this new role. I think you'll find much more satisfaction when you do."

Anthony needed to adapt his style for greater success as a board member and was fortunate that Anaka agreed to serve as a Think Out Loud partner. With her help, Anthony learned work modeling, and abandoned his long-held leadership role to now become an "advisor." He quickly grasped both the logical and emotional implications of this change, and the interdependencies and hotspots that were revealed:

Anthony

- The advisor role changed his relationships with both board and staff members
- What You Do remained a hotspot until Anthony realized his Key Activity was to offer experienced perspectives and recommendations, not directives
- Benefits Offered shifted from financial results to risk avoidance and strategic foresight

At subsequent meetings, other participants experienced Anthony as a greatly improved, contributing team member.

3. Ask the Three Questions

Whenever you sense a need for career change, the Three Questions can help you

(1) clarify what decision is needed, and

(2) define your best next steps. At those times, ask yourself:

1. Is it time to Move Up?

Is it time to progress to a new level—or maybe seek a promotion?

2. Is it time to Move Out?

Is it time to move out of a role, reporting relationship, team, organization, or profession that is no longer a good fit?

3. Is it time to Adapt Your Style?

If you like your work but are failing to enjoy the success you want, is it time to adapt your style?

Think of the Three Questions as an always-on navigation system that pinpoints your current career location—and where to travel next. The Three Questions can prevent you from impulsively quitting and seeking a new job, a decidedly non-strategic move that often results in merely relocating an unresolved career problem to a new workplace.

The Three Questions are comprehensive and cover all career actions available to you at any given time. Read on to learn how to use them.

CHAPTER 9

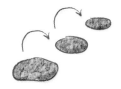

Ask Yourself the Three Questions

Ask Yourself the Three Questions

In Chapter 4 you learned to deal with "hotspots" by asking yourself the Three Questions:

1. Is it time to **Move Up?**
2. Is it time to **Move Out?**
3. Is it time to **Adapt Your Style?**

You also learned that the Three Questions can serve as a powerful navigation tool— almost like a GPS that pinpoints your current career location and shows you the best path forward. Like a GPS, the Three Questions serve as an ongoing tool for assessing your career trajectory. But few people regularly assess their careers in a conscious, deliberate manner, which too often means they react to circumstance rather than harnessing it. Harness circumstance to your advantage with a clear set of questions that quickly gets to the heart of a huge topic: *How am I doing career-wise?*

Responses to the Three Questions vary for everyone, but the point is that better questions trigger better thinking, and better thinking produces better decisions. As you get ready to use the Three Questions as a regular, conscious means of career assessment, here are two tips: 1) avoid "tornado thinking," and 2) welcome your intuition.

Cindy

Avoid Tornado Thinking

Cindy is a 49-year-old mother of two and a senior paralegal who also serves as general office manager for a busy law firm with 27 attorneys. For several years she has been spinning the same career-related thoughts around and around in her mind, without coming to any resolution or decisions:

> I'm as capable as most of our lawyers, should I go to law school? At my age? Not sure I really want to stay in the legal profession...But we can't really afford to lose my income now that the kids' college expenses are on the horizon...Still, I really love my new aromatherapy hobby and Janine says I could sell my products on Etsy...Maybe if Jim and I downsized I could turn it into a business??...

Cindy is experiencing a classic case of "tornado thinking." Like tornadoes that swoop up entire neighborhoods, swirl them through the air, then scatter the debris miles distant, we've all experienced "information tornadoes" that sweep up voices from the data landscape—hearsay, facts, fears, Internet news—then spin those voices around-and-around in our minds.

That mental discussion might stop when the phone rings or a child asks for help with homework.

But as in Cindy's case, ten minutes or hours or a day later, the same internal conversation bubbles up. The same mental debris begins spinning over-and-over again as we listen—without knowing how to make sense of it or make it go away.

Here's good news: like expert storm chasers, we can recognize that valuable information—even knowledge—is locked within a mental tornado. And we can recognize that tornado thinking indicates that urgent career questions need answering.

THE HOUSING AUTHORITY DIRECTOR

Herb

Welcome Your Intuition

Herb is a 61-year-old civil engineer who served as housing authority director for a smaller West Coast city for 28 years. He bonded with Skyler, a free-spirited 31-year-old department administrator, over their mutual love of sailing and sailboats.

The two regularly met for lunch and would sometimes commiserate about bureaucracy and the slow-moving nature of their own department. One day over coffee Skyler suddenly announced he was quitting.

"I'm going to register for that three-month boat-building course on the Normandy coast I told you about," said Skyler. "Guess I'll finally get around to improving my French!"

Skyler

Herb felt a ping of jealousy at Skyler's words, but quickly congratulated his colleague.

"You've got a lot of seniority here, Herb," Skyler continued in a friendly tone. "What's next for you?" He meant the words as a compliment.

But Herb felt vaguely judged by Skyler's question, and in the following days and weeks the *What's next for you?* query haunted him repeatedly. Meanwhile, his thoughts kept turning to the hand-built wooden sailboat that had lain half-finished in his garage for six years.

Herb recognized that this mental "tornado" pointed to an unresolved career issue, so he decided to welcome his intuition and talk things over with a thought partner. After sharing his thinking aloud with an empathetic former city manager, Herb realized it was time to retire.

Now, on most sunny days he can be found on the water—in his handbuilt sailboat.

Jeff

The Think Out Loud Laboratory

The Three Questions will help you avoid tornado thinking, engage your intuition, make decisions, and act. But accomplishing all this requires a "Think Out Loud Laboratory."

A Think Out Loud Laboratory is simply a conversation with someone you trust: a thought partner who listens and asks you questions *rather than compulsively offering advice*. A Think Out Loud Laboratory is what you need when you're grappling with questions that resist clear answers. It's a place to discuss other people's answers that you dislike, mistrust, or don't understand. It's a real place with real people, outside of your head. It's a place where you can sound curious or hear yourself say surprising—even naïve—things.

Sometimes a simple Think Out Loud Laboratory can quickly lead to resolution and action.

For example, Jeff was a 49-year-old lecturer in history at a liberal arts college who couldn't see himself working in the classroom for another 16 years. He had always been sought out by students for advice and counsel, so becoming a certified counselor felt like a logical and emotionally satisfying next career step. But his wife's words gave him pause. *You need a PhD to do your ideal job,* she had said. *Do you want to start that at age 49?*

After talking with colleagues and getting the facts about requirements for working as a counselor, Jeff discovered that a master's degree was adequate. Now it was time to Move Up: to progress by enrolling in a master's degree program in counseling.

Like Jeff, you may discover questions or answers from people around you (or in this book) that prompt intuitive reactions. Listen to those reactions quietly and carefully with your body as well as your mind. Feelings of discomfort are clues to something that needs further inquiry: a "hotspot," so to speak. Use the discomfort to better know the hotspot. And if the discomfort is too familiar, let that motivate you to design a different work model.

Why Think Out Loud Laboratories Work

Frank

Herb and Jeff show how Think Out Loud Laboratories work by bringing third-party objectivity to bear on career quandaries. But there's another reason why they work, too. As it turns out, thinking and talking involve two completely different brain processes. Most of us have experienced the striking difference between clarity of thought and clarity of speech during interviews.

Frank, for example, was a 58-year-old veteran of the Columbia River waterways. Over three decades he had worked his way up from deckhand to engineer to mate, and finally to tugboat captain, where he had spent 14 years navigating the river's entirety.

But Frank wanted to grow beyond "pushing barges," so he decided to seek the challenge, prestige, and higher salary that came with becoming a certified Columbia River Pilot. That status would allow him to pilot 100-ton and larger vessels, including foreign-flagged ships entering the Columbia from the Pacific Ocean. The certification required stringent written and oral interviews with the Columbia River Pilot Association—including a difficult, detailed map test.

"I memorized 280 miles of navigation aids and channel markers to prep for this," Frank proudly told a friend. But he neglected to practice verbally answering questions before appearing for the interviews and test.

The big day finally arrived. Following completion of the written portion of the exam, the lead interviewer complemented Frank on accurately reproducing a map of Columbia River navigation aids. Then he asked his first question. "Frank, tell us about a time you handled conflict among crew members while underway on the river."

I've got this question nailed, thought Frank. He immediately recalled an incident where his first mate and one of the deck hands nearly broke out in a fist fight during a heated argument.

"But then my mouth flew open and my answer fell apart," he remembers. "I said something

like, *We were pushing a three-barge load of wheat—well, it wasn't all wheat, there was some other grains and one barge of petrochemicals—but the weather was good and there wasn't much chop...*

"And it got worse," Frank sighed. "I started blathering: *We were approaching the Willamette confluence...*and blah, blah, blah. I rambled on without a word about handling crew conflict. I didn't know where I was going stop."

Frank had derailed. Despite his outstanding experience and competence, Frank made the classic interview mistake: failing to practice telling professional identity-linked accomplishment stories out loud to a trusted partner prior to the interview. As a result, he found himself scrambling to organize his thoughts and words.

Put simply, silently rehearsing something in your mind is completely different from *rehearsing it aloud. Equally important, rehearsing something aloud while you are alone is completely different from rehearsing it in the presence of another person.*

Like many of us, Frank over-relied on *thinking*—a silent cognitive process—and failed to prepare for his interview by using actual speech, which requires the mental rigor of one-to-one dialogue: converting thoughts into language clear and concise enough to be readily understood by others. When we convert our thoughts to spoken language, we discover additional energy, nuances of meaning, or values, *all based on how we sound when we say things aloud.*

What Frank discovered is precisely what you'll discover when you verbally describe your work model to another person.

Bear in mind that all of this applies, not just to those preparing for interviews, *but to anyone experiencing tornado thinking who has not yet verbally articulated their thoughts in the presence of another trusted person.*

P.S. Frank engaged a thought partner, practiced interviewing, and successfully passed the Columbia River Pilot Association interview and exam on his second attempt.

Mark

When Is It Time to Move Up?

Think of "moving up" as progressing along your own developmental curve, not necessarily rising in an organizational hierarchy in terms of status or compensation. Moving up could also mean:

1. Shifting laterally or even "down" in an organization to do work that represents your preferred next step in personal development, regardless of what your employer considers "next" to be

2. Developing in place by enriching your current role

3. Changing geographic location to broaden your experience

Mark is a 44-year-old healthcare executive who grew up in a family of doctors. He began university as a premed student, but in his late sophomore year developed a strong interest in finance, information technology, and organizational development and ended up graduating with an unusual double major in business and biology.

Mark's first job following graduation was as a junior financial analyst in the headquarters of a large regional hospital chain. He excelled in this role. Within two years he was promoted to senior financial analyst, then reached the rank of comptroller just three years later. It was then that he resolved to eventually become a hospital CEO in his dream city: San Diego. He began looking for work within the hospital chain that would provide both momentum and direction toward his goal, and started by diagramming his employer's service model, calling it a "hospital operating system."

Mark Moves "Down"

Colleagues were flabbergasted when Mark voluntarily left his comptroller position to take on a significantly less prestigious role: as project manager for the implementation of a new enterprise resource planning (ERP) platform that his employer believed would revolutionize the way equipment and supplies were bought, accounted for, and managed throughout its hospital chain. Though the move was a step down in terms of status and salary, Mark had resolved that whatever work he took on would *send* him somewhere rather than *keep* him somewhere.

Mark had foreseen that overseeing the ERP implementation would give him both change management skills and an unprecedented operational understanding of the entire hospital network—all *while making him known to executives at every hospital in the chain.*

In this sense, the ERP implementation was an ideal form of Outward Focus. He spent 18 months at a recently acquired midsize hospital overseeing the pilot implementation.

Mark Moves "Across"

Following the successful ERP implementation, Mark made another move to generate more momentum toward his goal of becoming a hospital CEO. Knowing that the new ERP system was slated for an enterprise-wide rollout the following year, he applied to become vice president of administration at a bigger, long-established hospital within the network, touting his track record in ERP implementation. His application was approved, and Mark made a lateral move that brought him closer to his goal.

The bigger hospital benefited from Mark's system implementation and leadership experience. Meanwhile, Mark gained credibility as an operational hospital executive. This role imparted even greater speed, momentum, and direction toward his goal.

Mark Moves Up

Mark finally arrived at his ultimate destination: he was promoted to CEO of the 280-bed flagship hospital in San Diego. In light of his artful moves it didn't surprise Mark, or others around him, that he had achieved his goal.

Each new work experience had given Mark added capability and credibility. His decisions were thoughtful and strategically timed. Each move showed him acting in a self-reliant way, proactively managing his work life as if he were self-employed: marketing himself to his current employer as though he were an outside consultant or contractor. He used the speed, momentum, and direction of each new role to move him toward his career goal and fulfill his "North Star" professional identity.

Few professionals possess Mark's foresight, skill, or patience implementing a career plan that spanned nearly a decade. But you now grasp two key principles that enabled Mark's success:

1. Understand the service or business model of your intended workplace

2. Make sure your work is *sending* you somewhere, not *keeping* you somewhere

When Is It Time to Move Out?

Gabriella

When is it time to move out of a supervisory relationship, job, organization, industry, or profession where the situation or the work itself no longer fits?

This question comes easily to people who either (a) feel confident they can improve their circumstances by competing in the open labor market, or (b) are so discouraged they feel they have nothing to lose by quitting their jobs. The rest of us hesitate to ask ourselves this question because moving out changes many aspects of life besides work.

Quitting to Find Herself

Gabriella is a 41-year-old human resources professional who majored in psychology during college and went on to become a family counselor. After several years of working as a counselor and therapist she earned a master's degree in organizational development, then took a series of human resources-related jobs in the private sector. At age 34 she found herself in Silicon Valley working in a training and development role for a company that makes scientific testing and measuring instruments.

"They were a progressive firm and everything moved fast. I thought they were on the leading edge of contemporary organizational development—it was very exciting," she remembers. "Then they executed a big restructuring, and I felt like the exciting times were over."

A chance meeting changed everything.

"During a business trip to the Pacific Northwest I met a recruiter at the hotel where I stayed," she recalls. "She took my business card and I forgot about it."

The recruiter remembered Gabriella, though.

"A few months later she called and told me about an opportunity to head up workforce development at a huge electrical utility in the Pacific Northwest," says Gabriella. "It meant a big jump in title and salary. I interviewed, got an offer, and took it."

Gabriella reflected on the transition with wisdom and humility.

"From day one I learned the hard truth of what it means to work in a public utility. They were saddled with a huge bureaucracy, and more than 30% of their employees were unionized, making human resources work a nightmare—like dealing with two completely separate workforces. And to top if off, they were in the middle of being bought out by another utility!"

Each workday became a struggle for Gabriella.

"It was around this time that I learned about business models—that was a real eye-opener. After diagramming my employer's model, I saw the trouble spots as clearly as fire at night.

"I experienced constant pit-of-the-stomach dread and a sense that I was lifting dead weight that would never come to life. I kept having talks with myself about 'trying harder'…'trying again'…'trying it another way'…All in all, it was a self-inflicted case of organizational-cultural whiplash," she admits. "I had been seduced by a lofty title and salary.

"Finally, I tried a thought experiment using the *Move up?* question: I looked at my situation like it was a bad movie, then fast-forwarded that movie, and asked myself, *What if things got so much better that I was promoted? Would I feel better at that next level up? Would I feel more aligned with my new colleagues?* The answers to all those questions was the same: No.

"That left two questions: *Adapt style? Move out?* Adapting my style would have been like changing myself from being right-handed to being left-handed. So, *Adapt my style?* was not the right question.

"That left *Move out?* And I realized I was facing a gravity problem: the organization wasn't going to change. The work and culture were a poor fit. It was *time to move out.*"

Fortunately, Gabriella had kept in touch with her network and was able to identify a new opportunity.

"I learned a valuable lesson about my work model requirements—the ability to creatively make a difference—and my *workplace model* requirements: no bureaucracy," she says.

Gabriella recognized two important reasons why she was able to move out.

"First, I didn't just stifle my intuitions. I used my doubts and concerns as motivation to diagram my employer's business model. I soon recognized hotspots that conflicted with my values and my work style. I couldn't live with those hotspots and I couldn't change them.

"Second, a think out loud lab with one of my Silicon Valley colleagues reminded me how valuable it is to maintain outward focus and keep network relationships alive so you can detect your next work opportunity."

When Is It Time to Adapt Your Style?

When things don't work out, or when someone is deemed "not a good fit" or "failing to step up to the level needed," very often it is due not to lack of skill or knowledge, but rather due to the style by which the person delivers their work.

Style | def.- a particular, distinctive, or characteristic mode of action or manner of acting

Style is a set of behaviors sought by employers when they are looking for "chemistry" or "soft skills" or "fit" with either their organizational culture or with a particular manager. Style is real, measurable, and important—yet most hiring managers and recruiters can only muster vague descriptions of what style means in terms of specific behavior.

That was not the case for Dembe, an up-and-coming manager in a new rural clinic that was part of a progressive hospital chain.

"I came to understand my leadership style so clearly when I went to work for a new, progressive healthcare company," says Dembe. "After my first year as a manager I received valuable feedback about my leadership style using a 360 assessment called Benchmarks. And my boss would attend some of the meetings and discussions that I led and give me real-time feedback about what she saw and heard. For example, *You only engage with talkative people, not necessarily the ones with the best ideas.*

Dembe

"She shared with all her direct reports results of our personality profiles that described, with shocking accuracy, how we tended to act in stressful and non-stressful situations. For example, I'm an extrovert so it's no wonder I pay too much attention to others like me who are outgoing.

"All of this gave me the words to describe my style and the insights to know when I needed to adapt it for certain situations. I realized that I was a better facilitator of decision-making than I was a decision-maker. Pretty important for a manager to know!"

Everyone adapts their style bit by bit and day by day. The trick is to know when to make a significant change. Knowing when the time is right calls for the courage to ask two key questions:

1. *Is it "me" rather than "them" who needs to adapt?*
2. *What is there about my own professional—or unprofessional—style that might be contributing to my discontent or lack of success?*

These are tough questions we fail to ask ourselves often enough. But both questions move you beyond assigning cause or blame to others around you, even when they may deserve it.

One indication that a style change is needed is personal interactions you initiate in the workplace are making you or others uncomfortable. One common example is jumping to offer solutions before fully understanding what other people are trying to articulate as problems they face. The reason for this may not involve anyone being "wrong." You may, in fact, need to change your style because you are more insightful or resilient than your colleagues and are therefore able to adapt to people less flexible or insightful than you. On the other hand, you might well benefit from outside perspectives on your style, such as a 360° evaluation or a frank discussion with your direct supervisor or human resources person.

Sometimes the only way to successfully handle a tough (or unfair) situation is to realize you're unable to change the underlying reasons, whether they involve organizational culture, a particular manager, market conditions, government regulations, or some other "gravity" problem. The only thing you control is the style by which you respond.

THE FINANCIAL ANALYST

Feedback Saves a Manager—and Her Project

Jill is a 38-year-old financial analyst who joined a large consulting firm after completing her MBA. She spent several years working in consulting, then joined a large sports footwear and apparel company in a financial planning role.

Like many companies in the highly competitive sportswear industry, Jill's employer needed to redesign operations for greater speed, so one of Jill's first assignments was to lead a change initiative to improve real-time financial information availability by implementing new software and processes. Jill's boss made it clear that, like most change initiatives, it would be rocky and painful at times—but the completion deadline was absolute and immovable.

Jill

Jill threw herself into the work, diligently putting in an enormous number of hours each week. But she soon became frustrated with many of the people working under her, who seemed compliant but unenthusiastic about the project. Within months this frustration grew to the point that Jill became visibly annoyed with what she perceived as lackluster engagement on the part of her own team members.

"After one particularly tough day at the office, I asked myself, *Is it time to move out of corporate finance?*" she

says. "Then I remembered Outward Focus and some hard-hitting lessons learned from a group feedback exercise we did during my MBA program and thought, *Maybe I'm the problem here.*"

Jill asked HR to design a feedback survey to discover what people truly thought about her leadership and the progress of her change initiative.

"The results showed I needed to adapt my leadership style if I was going to be successful," Jill remembers. "My colleagues saw me as only being interested in meeting the project deadline. Nobody felt that management cared about employee success in the future. That was a real wakeup call for me."

Jill admits she had become short-sighted and narrowly focused in her communications to colleagues. "I had forgotten to lead people all the way through problems—not just up to them—before moving on," she says.

Informed and motivated by the feedback, Jill adapted her communication style by spending more one-on-one time answering team member questions about their futures with the company. Her payoff was a successful project and a well-maintained reputation as a leader who inspired results rather than simply demanding them.

Are You Bold Enough?

Jot down the names of at least one former manager:

Are you bold enough to contact them and ask what style changes they wish you had made while working for them?

If you're really bold, ask your current boss what style changes they would like you to make—and in what specific situations. Specifics are essential: general statements about your style are rarely helpful, so ask for specific situations. If you can, it's best to have this conversation over an offsite lunch or breakfast.

The Three Commandments and Think Out Loud Partners

The cases in this chapter show people assessing fit between individual work models, organizational models, and professional identities. When the fit wasn't ideal, they posed the Three Questions to determine the best course of action. And by maintaining Outward Focus they were able to make informed choices about better-fit work, better-fit workplaces, and effective style adaptations.

They didn't do this important work alone in their minds. They reached out to others for feedback and "thought out loud" about their work. We call these trusted others Think Out Loud Partners—colleagues who are essential for good career management. Learn how to find the best partners for you in the final chapter.

Challenge Yourself with These Questions:

1 Which of the Three Questions speaks most strongly to me right now?

2 Have I discussed this question with a partner so I can discern which thoughts are assumptions and which are facts?

3 Fill in the blank: How can I move up if I don't know more about _____ ?

4 Should I move out of my current organization? Or is there a better-fit opportunity somewhere else within it?

5 Have I asked for feedback from workplace colleagues or supervisors?

Learn how to **find the best** *partners for you in the final chapter.*

CHAPTER 10

Find Your Think Out Loud Partner

Can You Hear You?

Eric, the systems engineer-turned-trainer whom you first met on page 96, smiled as he reflected on a recent phone conversation with François, a colleague who worked in the Montreal offices of EPIC, the electronic medical records firm.

Barely a year had passed since the two met in person during one of Eric's long business trips, yet Eric felt as though the travel-intensive stage of his career was a lifetime away.

"So how did you come up with this new training role for yourself?" François asked. "You must have been plotting this for some time."

"Quite the opposite," Eric replied. "I was stuck in tornado thinking—spinning work-related thoughts over and over in my head without resolving or deciding anything. My coach showed me a visual model that put those thoughts on paper and let me see my career objectively—and how it contributes to EPIC's operations. After that, the insights and connections almost made themselves."

There was a brief silence.

"Wow," François replied. "I might want to get this coach's contact information from you."

Earlier we described the challenges of reflecting on your work model alone. When reflection is completely internal, you are unable to truly "hear" yourself—or benefit from the transformative process of sharing your thoughts with another person.

That's why we recommend using a Think Out Loud Laboratory: a conversation space shared with a thought partner. But how to best find a trustworthy, objective person to invite into your Think Out Loud Laboratory? Let's consider some candidates and assess their advantages and disadvantages.

Manager or Key Partner at Work

Managers owe their livelihoods and their loyalty to your employer, so be careful here. They could experience conflict helping you either move up or away from their team if their productivity—or bonus—depends on ensuring key people like you remain in place. Even sympathetic key partners may find "move up" conversations awkward if they feel unable to provide you with a satisfactory path to career progress.

In progressive organizations that truly understand people management, you'll have no trouble initiating a conversation about your work model. In fact, your manager or mentor may initiate the conversation first! Such organizations are rare, so consider them excellent workplaces for gaining experience and testing new work models. Eric was fortunate to be employed at EPIC under a supervisor who saw the potential in his new model.

Friend/Colleague Who Moved Out, Up, or Adapted Style

People who have successfully moved up, moved out, or adapted their styles should populate your network: they can provide much of the personal feedback or market intelligence you need. While no one posseses an all-knowing perspective on market reality or your best career move, each can share a constructive view of your work model, and collectively they represent the current workplace climate.

The reason for meeting with such people is to avoid over-relying on your own perceptions. This is why career consultants push clients to talk with friends, colleagues, and colleagues of friends. Look for someone who poses good questions based on mature curiosity rather than a know-it-all convinced that their personal view represents the market view. Finally, choose someone willing to disagree with you or put forward a different opinion. A healthy challenge to your model or your perception of workplace needs sharpens your thinking—and your conversations with other thought partners.

Therapists

Therapists are a poor choice as thought partners regarding your work life. Why? The biggest reason is lack of experience in organizations unrelated to therapy. Becoming a therapist requires extensive academic study, internships, licensing, supervised clinical experience, plus mastering the intricacies of insurance reimbursement or government funding. Few therapists have significant exposure to business, diverse workplace cultures, or the broader spectrum of careers.

To their credit, most therapists recognize they are unsuited for career counseling, and instead will refer clients to career coaches after helping them reduce or manage anxiety, depression, or angry reactions to workplace situations. If you work with both a therapist and a career coach, ask them to talk with each other and exchange perspectives on how they engage with you. Too often therapists and coaches work in their own "silos" of incomplete perception about a particular client. You can benefit tremendously when information is shared among those who are striving to further your success.

Professor, Teacher, or Instructor

Professors, teachers, or instructors can be helpful when they know where former students went to work and either prospered or suffered. But their student interactions are usually limited to pre-graduation study, and they often enjoy little ongoing contact with students after they've entered the workforce.

One rich academic resource, though, is your college or university career center—and the staff there who can connect you to other alumni. Your fellow graduates work in thousands of different organizations, and you are an official member of this academic circle. Use this membership. Make contacts. If nothing else, it's a safe place to test your work model with people who are already favorably disposed toward you as members of the same academic "tribe."

Spouse, Partner, or Person You're Dating

Therapists and physicians don't treat their own families for the same reason you should avoid relying on spouses or partners for career-related thought partnerships: dual relationships are inherently conflicted and potentially unethical. You can't expect objectivity from someone who shares the most intimate aspects of your life. Go easy here: you're dealing with a source of unconditional emotional regard—someone who will support you when you need it most. Don't ask them to serve as a career resource.

What's more, if you've struggled over time with work-related frustrations, you may already have exhausted your spouse or partner's capacity to empathize with your career concerns. Instead, find another trusted person who knows your career territory and its possibilities. If possible, turn to a thought partner who has used tools in this book to manage their own career.

On Disagreeing with Thought Partners

A work model condenses information into a single diagram and enables you to test assumptions that went into its design. So, be bold enough to choose a thought partner who can challenge your model. Your partner is giving you a precious gift if they offer evidence as to why and how your design should differ. If they make different assumptions or disagree with parts of your model, investigate their comments for accuracy.

For example, Edward was a 61-year-old architect with 28 years of seniority at a large urban design firm that had created a successful niche in shopping center remodeling—which meant Edward's work had become somewhat routine and largely enabled by computer-assisted design. Thinking ahead, Edward designed a pre-retirement work model that assumed stepping down to part-time work for a few years so he could enjoy modest continuing income before retiring full-time. He shared his model with a colleague, Allen, and was dismayed by the response.

"I think you're making a risky bet to assume the firm will make part-time work available," Allen cautioned.

Edward disagreed but decided to verify Allen's observation. He quickly discovered there were no part-time senior roles in his firm. Meanwhile, he read a trade magazine article stating that the industry trend was to let senior architects retire early and hire newly graduated architects with superior computer skills. Edward revised his model—and started reading up on the pluses and minuses of early retirement.

Become a Thought Partner for a Less Experienced Person

One good way to create a thought partnership is to teach work modeling to a less experienced person—then serve as their thought partner. You'll help yourself, too, because there's no better way to master something than by teaching it to someone else (research shows that learners tasked with teaching a method achieve far better mastery than those who simply read about the method). And now that you understand our career reinvention method, you possess knowledge that can be extremely helpful to others. Don't underestimate how helpful you can be! Share your knowledge freely.

Our experience is that working professionals quickly grasp the method, eagerly embrace it, and are grateful for the opportunity to learn together with more seasoned thought partners. Teaching high school or college students is more challenging, though, particularly if they have never worked full-time and had the sobering experience of paying their own rent, food, and mobile phone expenses.

On the other hand, working with inexperienced students may give you an opportunity to transform someone's life, as Danny's story shows.

Danny Learns What Work Means

Danny

Danny faced bigger problems than most teenagers. One month before the 17-year-old was poised to graduate from an inner-city Cleveland high school, he became homeless.

Growing up in a broken household beset by poverty and alcohol problems, for years Danny had intermittently "couch surfed" at friends' homes. He always took pains to help out in the places he stayed, but his unstable living situation made it impossible to both attend school and find paying part-time jobs. He had no money for rent.

Fortunately, Danny went to see Mr. Thompson, an amiable career counselor well-versed in work modeling. Mr. Thompson introduced Danny to the Work Model Canvas and suggested that Danny write down what other people told him he does well. Danny listed "handy around the house" and "being mature and responsible."

Mr. Thompson pointed out that these qualities were important **Key Resources**. He then asked, *Who helps you?* Danny defined his **Key Partners** as parents of friends, teachers, and school counselors.

Next, Mr. Thompson asked, *Who do you help?* and *How do you help?* Danny answered that his "customers" were friends and parents of friends whom he had helped over the years by doing light home repairs, lawn mowing, cleaning, and housesitting.

Danny quickly saw that if he could find someone who needed ongoing handiwork or other help around the house, he might exchange that help for temporary living quarters until he was able to find paying work and a permanent living situation. He asked his **Key Partners** to serve as "channel partners" to help him find such a customer. They did.

Three years later, Danny was working in construction—and living in his own apartment.

"If it weren't for Mr. Thompson and work modeling, I can't imagine where I'd be," says Danny. "They showed me what work really means."

What Work Means

Danny learned priceless lessons from this experience.

He learned that work means helping other people get important things done.

He learned that work means providing others with benefits—with value—rather than merely spending hours executing proscribed tasks.

He learned that workplaces are systems with interdependencies that require people to cooperate.

Every young person deserves to learn these lessons about work while still in school—yet few do. Sadly, public school career education has been outmoded for decades because it is based on the fallacy that careers progress in a linear fashion, and therefore the appropriate way to proceed is based on a Plan > Execute paradigm. The truth is that for most people, careers progress in a non-linear fashion, and therefore the appropriate way to proceed is based on a Model > Test paradigm, as presented in this book.

Career education is outmoded worldwide, a conclusion we reached after more than a decade teaching the Business Model You® methodology to thousands of people in more than 30 countries, both on the ground and remotely. Unfortunately, that conclusion has been confirmed by educators, researchers, teachers, career consultants, and business-people in every country we've visited.

So, if you are lucky enough to teach, supervise, coach, or mentor young people, we hope you adopt our Diagram > Reflect > Revise > Test approach.

Four Career Stages

Wherever work takes you, it is helpful to know that people transition through four distinct stages as they progress in their careers. Keep in mind that *they may transition back and forth between the stages, especially as they reinvent work at different times of life.*

1. Dependent

New workers like Danny depend heavily on others. They must ask for guidance as they test their **Key Resources**—what they've learned in school or training. They are likely to focus on **Key Activities** in the workplace. An experienced worker may return to this stage when learning new skills, as Edward did when computer-assisted design was first introduced.

2. Independent

Workers who have developed expertise can act on their own. They require little guidance and can begin to advise others. They are more aware of and capable of contributing to individual, team, and enterprise Value Propositions, but they are less aware of the importance of **Key Partners**. On page 156 we saw how Eric had progressed to the *independent* level where he could train others to install complex electronic medical records systems. But Eric's boss was operating at the next stage: *interdependent.*

3. Interdependent

Experienced, competent workers use Outward Focus to see the workplace as a system comprised of interdependent elements and roles. They seek and give cooperation to ensure both team and personal success. They are keenly aware of the importance of **Key Partners** and treat colleagues as **Key Partners**—or even **Customers**. Eric's boss saw the bigger picture and kept organizational needs in mind when she said to Eric, *We need a pipeline of up-and-coming senior systems engineers.*

4. Adjournment

Veteran workers are ready to begin easing into retirement. They may wish to continue in their profession as advisors, mentors, or teachers, or start something completely new and return to the *dependent* stage with a fresh sense of curiosity, purpose, and learning.

For example, married couple Jana and Henri were both nursing professionals who retired at the same time. Jana continued in nursing at the *independent* stage as a healthcare instructor for the humanitarian nonprofit organization Mercy Corps. Henri, meanwhile, returned to the *dependent* stage by enrolling in a carpenter apprenticeship program.

Recognizing someone's stage—and thinking carefully about it before engaging with them—enables you to ask more helpful questions and provide gentle guidance toward their next stage of development. Maybe it's your turn to do exactly that!

Food for Thought

1 Who will you invite into your Think Out Loud Laboratory? What will you talk about? How will you help them?

2 Which interdependency in your work model is a "hotspot" source of pain or potential? It might involve you, a colleague, your boss, a partner, a community, or even a technology. Discuss it with a thought partner, then describe one action you could take to reduce the pain or exploit the potential.

3 What career stage are you in now: Dependent, Independent, Interdependent, or Adjournment? There is no "best" stage, only the stage that fits who you are today. Ask yourself, *Which of the Three Questions is most relevant to me at this stage?*

4 Recall from page 223 *that work should be sending you somewhere, not keeping you somewhere*. Do you feel ready to move to a different stage? Remember, going back-and-forth between stages is OK! Describe things you do now that could send you to a desired new role—or a new career stage.

The Final Word

Congratulations on completing *Business Model You: The One-Page Way to Reinvent Your Work at Any Life Stage!* We hope you will journey beyond intellectual understanding and internalize the method to create greater workplace satisfaction (or at least reduce workplace suffering!) for yourself and others.

In closing, we would like to gift you with the secret formula for life.

Are you ready?

You may want to sit down and brace yourself.

OK, here it is:

Life = Working + Loving

We can't help you with love, but we've done our best to help you with work. And when work goes well, the rest of life often falls into place.

Here's to modeling—and to reinventing work at whatever stage of life you find yourself.

Love,

Tim and Bruce

Creator Biographies

Dr. Timothy Clark, Author

Tim believes everyone can boost career satisfaction by grasping basic entrepreneurship and design principles. He began his career as a Japanese-to-English translator focused on technology news and subsequently founded a marketing research consultancy that served clients such as Amazon.com, Bertelsmann Financial Services, and Intel. Tim's own work model was transformed when his firm was acquired by a NASDAQ-listed corporation, an experience that inspired him to formally study and teach entrepreneurship. He became a professor of business and authored, co-authored, or edited eight books on entrepreneurship and personal development, including the global bestsellers *Business Model You* and *Business Model Generation.* A Stanford graduate, Tim also earned MBA and doctorate of business degrees and became a NEXT-certified entrepreneurship trainer.

Bruce Hazen, M.S., Author

Author Bruce Blackstone Hazen (*Answering the Three Career Questions, Business Models for Teams,* and *Business Model You*) is a career and management coach who has guided leaders and followers to bespoke answers to the Three Career Questions for over two decades. His mission is clear: reduce suffering at work, increase career satisfaction, and prevent careers from being spent finding one-job-in-a-row. He brings his "New Physics of Career Management" to this new edition of *Business Model You.* Previously Bruce served in multiple leadership roles in both commercial and noncommercial enterprises in the technology, healthcare, energy, and professional service sectors. He graduated from Cornell University in industrial and labor relations and holds a graduate degree in clinical psychology.

Luigi Centenaro, Author of Chapter 7

Luigi pioneered the application of design thinking to personal branding and founded BigName, the people and team innovation specialists. He serves as lecturer on Personal Branding and Professional Innovation at top international business schools and is the lead developer of the Professional Innovation Toolkit, which includes the Personal Branding Canvas. An enthusiastic Business Model You® Certified Practitioner, he has facilitated hundreds of workshops around the world.

Mercedes Hoss, Methodology Co-Creator

Mercedes is a key co-creator of the Business Model You® methodology who has organized and co-facilitated dozens of Certified Practitioner trainings. She is an accomplished coach and facilitator and designs Corporate Talent Development and Team Dynamics Programs using Business Model You® and Business Model for Teams, often in combination with LEGO® SERIOUS PLAY® and other methodologies.

Keiko Onodera, Designer

Following graduation from Kuwsawa Design School in Tokyo, Keiko joined the R&D division at foodmaker Yukijirushi, where she was awarded prizes for her innovative designs. She then joined cosmetics giant Shiseido to design products and packaging. She moved to the U.S. in 1991 and worked with design firm UCI, then co-founded an online marketing consultancy where she designed Japanese language websites and marketing research programs for clients such as Amazon.com, JCPenney, and Neiman Marcus. Today she works as an independent designer.

Community

Visit the free Business Model You® community site to download tools from the book, read posts and articles, access other resources, and meet thousands of other like-minded professionals from around the world.

Community.BusinessModelYou.com

Find a Certified Practitioner

Looking for a coach, consultant, or counselor who is an expert in the Business Model You® methodology? Visit the free directory of Certified Practitioners and search by language, location, and professional background to find your perfect thought partner!

BMYDirectory.com

Certified Practitioner Training

If you have been struck by the power and effectiveness of the Business Model You® method in your own life—and are thinking of using it to help colleagues or clients—consider becoming a Certified Practitioner. In seven immersive sessions, you will master the methodology as taught by its founder and learn to apply it in your own professional practice. What's more, you'll enjoy powerful feedback from like-minded colleagues working in a range of industries, giving you additional insights into how you can use the method both within organizations and as an independent professional.

PractitionerTraining.org

Citations

CHAPTER 1

1 The tree metaphor is adapted from *Who's Running Your Career? Creating Stable Work in Unstable Times*, by Caela Farren (Bard Press, 1997), an extraordinarily insightful and prescient work on career development.

2 Roy F. Baumeister, *Meanings of Life* (Guilford Press, 1992).

CHAPTER 2

3 Alexander Osterwalder and Yves Pigneur, *Business Model Generation*, (Hoboken, NJ: John Wiley & Sons, 2010). This is the standard work on business modeling for which author Clark served as contributing co-author and general editor.

4 Visit Strategyzer.com to download the Business Model Canvas and learn about other useful enterprise modeling tools.

5 D.H. Meadows and D. Wright, *Thinking in Systems: A Primer* (Chelsea Green Publishing, 2015).

6 A negative externality is a cost affecting people who did not choose to incur that cost, such as air pollution that diminishes public health or property values. Free public education is often considered a positive externality because educated citizens tend to make society more stable and productive, even for people without children.

CHAPTER 3

7   See Clare Winnicott, *Face to Face with Children: The Life and Work of Clare Winnicott* (Routledge, 2019) for a discussion of how social workers have used "third things" or "third objects" as forms of shared experience from which powerful communication can emerge.

CHAPTER 4

8   Bruce Hazen, *Answering the Three Career Questions: Your Lifetime Career Management System* (CreateSpace, 2013).

9   Alain de Botton, *The Pleasures and Sorrows of Work* (Pantheon, 2009).

10 Ibid.

11 Cal Newport, *So Good They Can't Ignore You* (Grand Central Publishing 2012).

12 Bill Burnett and Dave Evans, *Designing Your New Work Life* (Vintage 2021).

13 Ibid.

14 Ibid.

15 Ibid.

CHAPTER 5

16 W. Chan Kim and Renée Mauborgne, *Blue Ocean Strategy* (Harvard Business Review Press, 2015).

CHAPTER 6

17 See Steve Blank's work, including *The Startup Owner's Manual: The Step-By-Step Guide for Building a Great Company* (Wiley, 2020) for a comprehensive treatment of the Customer Development Model and related topics.

18 Ibid.

CHAPTER 7

19 Luigi Centaro is the creator of the Personal Brand Canvas and authored Chapter 7 of this book.

CHAPTER 8

20 The authors are grateful to Wayne Kittelson, founder of Kittelson & Associates, for sharing his comprehensive Outward Focus philosophy as applied to commercial enterprises. Mr. Kittelson considers Outward Focus a common element of many great spiritual traditions and takes no credit for creating it, though the extraordinary success and longevity of his company shows he is a master practitioner of the philosophy.

Index